The One Who Moves Mountains

ISBN: 978-0-9970115-5-5
eISBN: 978-0-9970115-6-2

Printed and bound in the United States of America.

The One Who Moves Mountains

ANDREA L. JOHANSON

DEDICATION

My beloved, Brian, there's no one I'd rather move mountains with than you! This book has been written with you as we've lived it together. Thank you for your constant belief in me and for your abiding love. So much more adventure awaits us!

> ". . . Let's praise the Lord together. Let's make him famous! Let's make his name glorious to all." (Psalm 34:3 TPT)

ACKNOWLEDGEMENTS

I'm incredibly thankful that I haven't walked this path of life alone and I'm especially grateful for each of the amazing family members and friends who have walked with me!

Besides my husband, our kids have been the ones who have most closely been part of this journey. I can't thank them enough for believing with us and standing in faith, even when the mountains have seemed overwhelming. Luke, Abbie, Noah, Nehemiah, I love you beyond words and believe in you with all my heart! You have such incredible destinies!

Daughter-in-law, Haley, and son-in-law, Thomas, thank you for saying yes – to Jesus and then to our son and daughter! You bring your own mountain-moving qualities to our family!

Peter and Masha Oswalt, our lives have been on a ridiculously accelerated path of healing and growth in God's kingdom since we met you. Your friendship has brought redemption to so much in our lives. Thank you for always saying "Yes" every time we invite you into our latest battle, and thank you for lighting a fire underneath me to get this book published!

For over three decades, my much-loved mother-in-law, Ritva Johanson, has covered our family in prayer. We wouldn't be where we are right now without that prayer covering. The majority of those years, she was joined in prayer by the sweetest, kindest man I've ever met – my father-in-law, David Johanson. I will forever be grateful to them both!

Last, but not least, I want to thank my friend, editor, and publisher, Rhonda Fleming. Long before this book was written, she believed in me and encouraged me as an author. I'm deeply grateful for her support, encouragement, wisdom, and help that have all made the publishing of this book possible!

My heart's desire has been to be God's quill, scribing for the Lord whatever's on His heart to share. All glory belongs to Him!

CONTENTS

INTRODUCTION

"I want your faith."

How many times has someone said that to me and I've wondered what on earth they could be talking about? Isn't a person who has incredible faith someone who speaks to mountains and they move? What I see are my failures – all the times I've spoken to mountains and only seen them loom larger than ever. I see all the times I've fallen short and the sleepless nights filled with anxious thoughts followed by stress-filled days . . . . Can you relate?

Yet, when I stop to think about it, I surprise myself with the realization that I *have* grown in my faith as I've learned to embrace the transformation process rather than fight it. Along the way, I've discovered so much about the truth of God's character – He *really is* who He says He is, I can stand on those truths, and I can hold Him to it. Even when I doubt Him, I've found it doesn't change who God is or how much He loves me.

I've also learned God really does see and hear me. I haven't been abandoned or forgotten by Him, which has been something I've often questioned and *needed* to be certain about, especially when times have been the most challenging.

Somewhere along the way, I realized I had to take ownership of mistakes that were clearly of my own doing and not shift the blame to God or others for things that were squarely resting on *my* shoulders. No one was more surprised than I was when it dawned on me that I had offense in my heart toward God. But once I realized it, I was able to ask His forgiveness and release things that had prevented me from being able to move forward in my faith because I had been stuck in a miry pit of anger and accusation.

One of my greatest discoveries has been learning I can have conversations with God and those conversations can include asking Him hard questions that can sometimes sound more like accusations. I've railed at God about my circumstances more times than I can count. I used to feel guilty and ashamed when I did, but then I realized God is big enough to handle my rants, so I stopped holding them in and laid them all out before Him.

By the time my energy was spent crying out to Him, I discovered my heart had been drawn more deeply to His, truth had broken through my thinking and, at some point, had renovated my soul. What had begun as plaintful pleas had transformed into declarations of truth, praise, and gratitude, and my journal entries seemed more reminiscent of David's psalms than tirades.

I know I'm not the only one walking a path like this because it's one traveled by countless others. The amazing thing is, as we travel together, we can learn from one another along the way, grabbing hold of truths we need to hear. As we do, it refreshes our souls and empowers us to put one foot in front of the other, each of us moving forward in all God has called us to be and do in our lifetimes.

It's my hope that as you turn the pages of this book, it will be as if our paths have intersected and we're chatting while walking side-by-side. Then somewhere along the way, you'll discover our conversation has turned into one between you and God. The thing is . . . God is ALWAYS speaking, and He wants to speak to *your* heart. When you engage Him in conversation, then listen, He *will* respond.

With that in mind, I've included some **Conversation Starters** at the end of each chapter that are intended to lead you into asking God additional questions of your own. Here are a few ideas for ways you can use the **Conversation Starters**:

- Grab your journal and write responses to each question, including what you believe you've heard God say in reply.
- Incorporate the questions into a conversational prayer time with God.
- Use them in a small a group setting with each person sharing their thoughts and the responses they heard God speak to their hearts.

If you've never had a conversation with God before and heard Him speak to you, no worries! We're going to talk more about that in just a bit. I have no doubt you'll soon find yourself chatting back and forth with the God of the Universe, the One who loves you more than you can possibly imagine!

In the meantime, grab a cup of tea or coffee, curl up in your favorite chair, and let's have a conversation about *The One Who Moves Mountains*.

CHAPTER 1

My Plan . . . Or His?

When I stop to think of mountains we've faced as a couple and as a family, I'm reminded how utterly terrifying and daunting some of those mountains have been.

More times than I could possibly count, I've asked God, "WHY?!? Our lives are surrendered to You. We've done our best to serve You. Our faith is placed in You. WHY have we gone through, and continue to go through, incredible challenges in our lives? *Where are You?* Have You abandoned us? Where are we missing it?"

Have you ever asked God similar questions?

Those queries often feel weightier as your kids get older and start to question their faith in God and His goodness because they see their parents STILL waiting on answers and breakthroughs they've believed Him for . . . for years . . . or even decades!

Can you relate?

These are just parts of our story . . .

- Health issues that have resulted in my husband, Brian, nearly dying multiple times.
- Financial struggles that have left us crying out for miracles that would keep us from getting evicted.
- Praying for creative ways to bring in money so the utilities stay on and we have food in the fridge.
- Selling my engagement ring and having garage sales to make ends meet.
- Owing family and friends money.
- Never yet having owned a house, only renting, and finding ourselves in the position of having to move to a new rental with no money for the deposit or first month's rent and having no clue how God was going to provide.
- Parenting challenges we somehow thought we'd be exempt from because we'd raised our kids according to Christian principles.

My own personal story also includes having been sexually abused by three different individuals between the ages of two and eleven, having my parents go through a bitter divorce by the time I was two, growing up with my mom being mentally ill and an alcoholic, my dad finally gaining custody of me when I was five, and him bringing me full-time into the blended family he had made with my step-mom. Their marriage was incredibly stormy, so home never really felt like a safe haven for me as a child.

My story isn't really all that different from others' and it's actually far better than what many have endured. The details in our stories vary, but we all have a past that, if we allow it, can be redeemed by the unconditional, sacrificial love of our Savior.

Through the ages, stretching back to the beginning of time, people have faced trials. All throughout scripture, in both the Old and New Testaments, we read about our favorite biblical characters walking through challenges of their own. Some of those challenges are still familiar to us today, whereas others, not so much. For instance, many today still struggle with infertility, but most of us haven't been thrown into a lion's den. Let's chat a bit about a crazy "love triangle" found in the Bible and see some ways we actually can relate to what our forefathers experienced.

Recently, I was reading Genesis 15 and 16, which talks about Sarai, the wife of Abram, coming up with a plan that, in her mind, would bring about the fulfillment of God's promise to her husband. I don't know about you, but I can totally relate to Sarai. She knew what God had promised and she saw a solution she thought could make it happen. I can't even begin to tell you how many plans I've come up with, and even implemented, that were *my* solutions for *God's* promises. Those have never worked out well for me. It didn't for Sarai either.

You probably know the story already. God had promised Abram countless descendants. But there was one problem – Sarai was barren. They were childless. Abram's solution was to leave all of his wealth to a servant who had been born in his house, which was the custom in that day if you didn't have a child of your own.

God actually came to Abram in a vision and said to him, *"Do not be afraid, Abram. I am your shield, your exceedingly great reward"* (Genesis 15:1b). Abram's response is a fantastic example of God being okay with us asking Him hard questions and engaging Him in conversation. Years prior to this, God had already promised Abram children of his own, but it was yet to happen. God then comes to Abram, tells him not to be afraid (which I'm sure God wouldn't have said if Abram wasn't dealing with a heck of a lot of fear at that time), told Abram who He was, but failed to mention anything about the fulfillment of the specific promise He'd made to Abram all those years before.

Gotta love it when God talks to you about everything BUT what you want Him to tell you more about! Abram held God to His promise and turned the topic of conversation to that sore point.

> But Abram said, "Lord God, what will You give me, seeing I go childless, and the heir of my house is Eliezer of Damascus?" Then Abram said, "Look, You have given me no offspring; indeed one born in my house is my heir!" (Genesis 15:2-3)

Ahhh. Abram had God's attention, God had his, and the conversation between the two continued from there. God wants us to engage Him in conversation. He wants us to remind Him of His promises to us. It's not because He's forgotten what He's promised, but reminding Him can be our declaration of faith and of what we know to be true.

4

I've leveled plenty of toddler-like accusations at God that have begun with, "But, YOU SAID . . . !" But I've also had plenty of faith-filled proclamations of, "You SAID . . . ! The latter has definitely been far more productive in moving toward the fulfillment of His promises!

Back to Abram and Sarai . . . .

God's response to Abram was to not only speak truth to Abram — "This one shall not be your heir, but one who will come from your own body shall be your heir" (Genesis 15:4). But in the very next verse he reiterated His promise to Abram and gave him something tangible — the stars — that would daily declare to him that God would be faithful to fulfill His word. "Then He brought him outside and said, 'Look now toward heaven, and count the stars if you are able to number them.' And He said to him, 'So shall your descendants be'" (Genesis 15:5).

Those stars . . . . God knew every time Abram walked outside at night, he would come face to face with countless reminders of God's promise to him. In Abram's day, there were no cities filled with electric lights that obscured the splendor of the night sky. It must have been incredibly awe-inspiring to see what Abram saw every single night! God knew that each pinprick of light would be a whisper from His heart to Abram's, reminding him, *"One who will come from your own body shall be your heir"* (Genesis 15:4).

God will often use the most ordinary things to be constant reminders of His promises to us.

As for Abram, he had a choice in that moment. He could either believe God and take Him at His word, even though it looked utterly impossible that God could fulfill His promise, or Abram could choose not to believe. It was a defining moment and one we can each find ourselves in any number of times throughout our lives. *Will we take God at His word and continue to wait? Or will we walk away in disappointment, believing it's impossible?*

Thankfully, Abram chose to believe.

God then took it a step further and "cut covenant" with Abram, which was His way of telling Abram that this was His unbreakable promise – not only to Abram, but to all his descendants who would come after him. (Genesis 15:7-21)

Now, enter Sarai . . . .

While it's not specifically written out in the Bible, I'm certain Abram came back to his tent and told Sarai all about this experience with God. How could he not? It was pretty monumental and not something easily forgotten. Plus, she had a rather important role to play in the fulfillment of God's promise, since she was Abram's wife and would therefore be the mother of the son God had promised him.

Bless Sarai's sweet heart. Month after month, year after year, she didn't see that promise being fulfilled. So, she figured out a plan to help God out. Oh, how I get her! How many times have I determined that the God of the universe needed MY help?

Sarai decided that her maidservant, Hagar, could be used as her stand-in to produce a son for her. She suggested that

Abram make Hagar his concubine so she could conceive a son in Sarai's stead. (Genesis 16:1-3) A concubine was a slave who filled the role of secondary wife and surrogate. She had no dowry, and no bride price was paid to her father. Concubines didn't hold the same status as primary wives, but they did earn a higher status than other concubines if they bore sons. It may sound crazy, but Sarai's plan was acceptable in those days and culture. So, Abram agreed, especially since the plan came from his wife.

Here's the thing. We wives can be VERY convincing. Lord, forgive me for all the times I've led my husband down a path other than Your best one for us! We can also truly believe that the plans we devise are God's solutions. Now, we don't have the only corner on that market. Husbands can do the same. All I'm saying is that I'm incredibly thankful for the ways my husband has grown over the years. Now he's much better able to help me discover that I may not necessarily have God's plan in mind when I'm pushing for a solution. Lord, I'm grateful for that man!

As the story goes, Abram took Hagar as his second wife and she had no problem conceiving. Because of that, she got a bit big for her britches and looked down on Sarai for being barren. Let's just say Sarai didn't take kindly to that. What did Sarai do? *She blamed her husband.* Remember – Sarai was the one who came up with this plan in the first place!

How often do we do that? We shift blame onto others for something that's a result of decisions *we* made. Sometimes we don't realize what we're doing and other times it seems far easier to shift the blame than to own up to the consequences of our personal choices.

Abram's response to Sarai was to tell her to do whatever she wanted to do with Hagar – she was her servant. (What happened to her also being Abram's *wife, slave or not*? Asking for a friend.)

Sarai was so harsh with Hagar that Hagar fled, planning to return to her home country, Egypt, but not really having a plan of how to get there. Who found her along the way? An angel, whom Hagar saw interchangeably as God Himself – as a manifestation of Him. (Genesis 16:6-7)

Even when we're on the run, God pursues us and finds us. He *knows* us. He called Hagar by name and even identified her as Sarai's maid. (Genesis 16:8) He knows each one of us by name and even knows the number of hairs on our head! Just as God pursued Hagar in the wilderness, He pursues us. Why? *Because of His love for us.*

Abram and Sarai took a bit of a detour when they came up with their own plan, but God still honored His promise to Abram. Hagar was pregnant with Abram's child and, because of that, God's promise stood firm. The Angel of the Lord told Hagar to go back to Sarai and He assured Hagar that He would *". . . multiply (her) descendants exceedingly, so that they shall not be counted for multitude"* (Genesis 16:10).

He went on to tell her about the son she was carrying and told her to call his name Ishmael. Now, I don't know about you, but I've always thought about Ishmael being synonymous with *making a mistake*. Admonitions of "You don't want to create an Ishmael!" ring in my ears from years past.

But did you know that Ishmael's name actually means "God hears"? The reason he was named Ishmael was not because he was a mistake, but because God had heard Hagar's troubles. (Genesis 16:11) When I discovered that, all I could think about was, in the midst of the messes we make, God hears what we're going through. Not only that, He can take any situation and bring good out of it *and bless us in the midst of it.*

That doesn't mean things are suddenly going to be easy. Things were never good between Sarai and Hagar. And it went from bad to worse as Ishmael grew older, ultimately resulting in Hagar and Ishmael leaving when he was a teen. (Genesis 21:8-21) Hagar still had a challenging road to travel, but her encounter with God transformed her. And I believe it enabled her to not only follow God's leading, but also gave her the strength and grace to live each day as a maid in Sarai's household.

What made the encounter such a crucial moment in time for her? She saw God and got a revelation of who God was, calling Him "You-Are-the-God-Who-Sees (El Roi); for she said, 'Have I also here seen Him who sees me?'" (Genesis 16:13).

That's what makes the difference! We can walk through *anything* and have faith in the midst of really hard times when we grab hold of the truth of who God is to us. When Hagar encountered God, she felt known and seen. She knew she wasn't alone, hadn't been forgotten, and wasn't abandoned. The God of the Universe saw her in the midst of her troubles, met her in that place, reminded her of His promises, and blessed her. That was all she needed. She could take her next steps forward because, not only did she have a revelation of His identity, but she also had a revelation of her own identity in Him.

Conversations with God, like the ones Abram and Hagar had, are available to each one of us. God loves to share His thoughts with us, and He wants us to share ours with Him (even though He already knows what we're thinking). It's not hard or mystical. It isn't something that's only available to the super spiritual or to priests or to those in ministry. It's not just available to a few people. He wants to be in conversation with each one of us!

Relationship (and by default, relating and conversing) is super important to God. It's so important to Him that when that relationship was broken by Adam and Eve and sin entered the world, separating us from Him, God already had a plan in place to restore right relationship with Him through the redemptive work of His Son, Jesus.

Here are some important things to know when you begin initiating conversation with God. First, know that God's words to you will always be loving, affirming, and kind. Anything that comes to your mind that's contrary to that isn't from the heart of God, especially if those words produce shame in any way. God may bring conviction to our hearts at times, but His words are never condemning, Second, while you may think you're going to hear the audible voice of God, that's usually pretty rare for people and, more often than not, His voice sounds a lot like yours in your head.

The Apostle John talks about sheep knowing the voice of their shepherd and how they never follow the voice of a stranger because they don't recognize his voice. (John 10:1-5) As you begin having regular conversations with God, trust you'll recognize His voice and He'll help you discern when it's your voice you're hearing or the voice of the enemy speaking lies.

If you have someone you trust in your life who has their own conversations with Jesus, share with them some of what you believe you're hearing God say. When you do, they may be able to confirm what you believe you're hearing from God and help you grow in confidence as you learn to recognize His voice.

Last tip. When you ask God a question, go with the first thing you hear. Then ask Him another question about that, especially if it seems to make no sense initially. Ask the next question that makes sense, listen for His answer, and go forward from there. I personally find it helpful to journal my conversations with Him, but do what works best for you.

Let's give it a try! Here are some **Conversation Starters** you can begin with related to this chapter.

1. Picture yourself standing with God, hands open before you. Ask Him, "What do you want me to give you in this season that I'm in?" Maybe it's disappointment or a job or a failure you believe you've had or something that's really good. Once you've heard what to give Him, then ask Him, "What are you giving me in exchange?"
2. As you wait on your promises from God, ask Him, "What are the 'stars' you're giving me as a constant reminder that You will fulfill your promise to me?"

3. In the midst of whatever you may be walking through, ask God to meet you there. Picture yourself with Him and ask Him, "What do you want to say to encourage me in this moment?"

CHAPTER 2

Wrestle with Me

God never promised us a pain-free life simply because we're faith-filled. As a matter of fact, Jesus told us just the opposite. "In this life you will have trouble . . . " (John 16:33 NIV). The good news is found in the second half of that verse where He says, "But take heart! I have overcome the world." When you have that truth deeply rooted within you and you truly believe it, you can stand in faith in the midst of the troublesome things of life.

Before we go any further, let's set the record straight. Yes, God is powerful and we will all stand before Him on Judgement Day. But He doesn't bring bad things into our lives to punish us for our sins or to test us in our faith or to cause us to grow in Him. That statement may be in direct opposition to what you've always thought or been taught. But if you read the New Testament, which was written after Jesus' death and resurrection, you read things like, ". . . If God is for us, who can be against us?" (Romans 8:31).

The Bible is very clear about who causes suffering in our lives. Satan is the one who has come to steal, kill, and destroy – *not* God. (John 10:10)

This may be hard to wrap your brain around, but God is *good*. He's a *loving* Father who wants to give us good gifts. For many, that picture is hard to accept because you've experienced an earthly father who is far from loving. Your dad may have been harsh, demanding, punitive, controlling, or abusive (or all of the above), and that's colored your perception of the Almighty God of the Universe who's also called Heavenly Father.

In many ways, things on earth are a representation of things in heaven, but we must remember that what's on earth has been marred by sin and man's will. Mankind is the only being God created with free will and, from the Garden of Eden on, man hasn't managed that gift well. The consequences of choices made by our ancestors in times past affect us even today. But we get to choose whether we're going to continue that legacy or establish a new one. I'm getting ahead of myself. Let me explain by sharing a bit of my early story.

Growing up, I always knew I was fiercely loved by my dad. He was extremely protective, and I knew he would likely literally kill anyone who seriously hurt me. That's one of the reasons I never told him I had been sexually abused. I fully believed that if I did and if he ever found out that two of the perpetrators were family members, he'd probably shoot to kill and go to jail. Now, that may not have happened, but I was convinced enough to keep silent.

While I knew I was deeply loved, I also had a healthy fear of my dad. He yelled – a lot. I grew up never feeling like I could fully please him (oh, how I tried) and that I was always just shy of the mark he'd set for me. As I grew older, I walked a fine line between being extremely proud of being a "Dunn" and hating carrying the name, because heaven forbid I make a mistake that tarnished said name. Whether or not that was true, that's how I felt.

Daddy was a self-made man. He was an illegitimate child, born in 1933, when that simply was not acceptable. He was orphaned by the time he was eight, bounced around from one alcoholic relative to the next, and was working by the time he was 11 years old. As an adult, he was a salesman, a private investigator, a lawyer, and ultimately a judge. He did tremendous good in the field of law and was highly respected, as well as somewhat feared. Lawyers knew that if they were appearing before him, they'd better be on time, look sharp, have their ducks in a row, and be fully prepared . . . or they'd certainly be dressed down and possibly dismissed if they weren't! Imagine growing up with him as your dad!

In recent years, I've come to the place of being able to see how the wounds he suffered as a child shaped him into who he became as a man, particularly in his drive to make a name for himself and to have his family uphold that name. It's given me tremendous compassion and the ability to forgive him for any pain he caused me. As the oft quoted adage goes, "Hurt people hurt people." That was my dad.

Forgiveness is a powerful tool for setting yourself free from the things that bind you. When you harbor unforgiveness toward someone, the only person it hurts is you. HONEST. I know how hard it can be to forgive! I know it can come down to it being a choice, an act of my will, and can have nothing to do with my emotions.

When I lead with my emotions in situations where forgiveness is needed, it's never a good thing. I become the judge's daughter and the person is found guilty, convicted, and sentenced to life imprisonment. The thing is . . . they aren't aware of the sentence I've rendered and they go about their lives, free from what I want them to suffer. I'm the one left angry and stewing over it for a lifetime. Their sentence becomes mine as I become trapped behind the bars of my own fury and indignation.

Having forgiven my dad doesn't mean I've forgotten what it was like growing up, but it's enabled me to realize he was doing the best he could based on his own woundedness and lack of truly knowing his identity in Christ. I've been able to embrace the incredible legacy he left in my life – one of valuing hard work along with the ability to persevere, always giving my very best in everything I do, and carrying a mantle of justice that seeks to right injustices in the world around me. He taught me to love hard and he instilled in me the value of family and of passing traditions on to future generations. That has very much shaped me in my role as a mom.

I will say there were also a lot of things I wanted to do differently as a parent. Remember I said earlier that we get to choose whether we're going to continue a family legacy or create a new one? When Brian and I got married, we determined there were things from our families we were going to incorporate into our marriage and there were ways we were going to very intentionally create a new legacy we hoped would be lasting throughout our future generations.

Brian grew up in a home in which there was no divorce; my family was riddled with it. We determined that, for us, our marriage would be built on three rules: Jesus Christ is Lord of our lives, divorce would never be an option so we would work it out when things got tough, and when we argued, we would never assassinate the other's character. We would focus on the issue at hand and not call each other names or declare "you always" or "you never" when we were at odds with one another.

For both of us, it would be a first that we would have a home in which our children would grow up knowing the love God had for them from the womb on. We purposed to take the best of the parenting we received growing up and to do the hard work within ourselves that was needed for us to become the parents God created us to be for our children.

Each time I had a baby, I would hold them in my hands, look at them, and know I was holding destiny. It was an awe-inspiring moment for me every time, especially knowing God had entrusted me to "train up" each child in the way they should go and, as a result, when they were older, I fully believed they wouldn't depart from it, because that's what God had promised me in His Word (Proverbs 22:6). That didn't mean they wouldn't stray along the way, but that's a conversation for another time.

We've done a good job as fallible parents who have made lots of mistakes along the way, and we have great kids who are an incredible blessing and who transform the world around them through God's call on each of their lives. AND . . . we've walked through rough times as a family, despite all of our efforts to create a "perfect" world for our kids. I've come to realize that I was living in a fantasy world when I dreamed of how our life would play out as a family, simply because we'd raised our kids with Christian principles as our foundation and tried to live as examples for our children with Christ at the center of our lives.

Never in my wildest dreams would I have anticipated the massive repercussions that Brian's health issues would have on our kids. From our financial struggles to the instability caused in their spirits and souls by living with a dad who walked through life-threatening illnesses all of their lives, they were left wondering why the God who heals hasn't healed their dad yet.

As much as I tried to protect our children's spirits from being wounded by others, and no matter how hyper-aware I was of protecting them from sexual abuse, I couldn't protect two of them from being bullied at school and suffering the repercussions from it for many years.

Having had three, picture-perfect pregnancies in a row, it never occurred to me that I would miscarry, not once, but twice, and would have to walk through the agony of soul that followed.

Our family's faith-filled world was rocked early on when our then pastors lost their seven-year-old child in a freak accident at an amusement park. He was our oldest son's best friend and was only a month younger than our daughter. His mom and I were pregnant together and our kids grew up side-by-side, with him being like another son to me.

I asked countless times in the midst of all of this, "God, where were You? WHY did you let this happen?" It was the same question I asked Him when I began the initial healing process I walked through when God began to heal me from the sexual abuse I endured.

If God is good and loving, why would He allow the troubles He promised we would face? I've been angry with Him plenty of times and held offense in my heart toward Him for both the big and the small, including multiple prayers that seemingly have gone unanswered.

I won't pretend to have all of the answers. I don't believe we'll ever fully understand this side of heaven some of the things we've walked through in our lives. What I do know is that God created man with self-will, sin exists in this world, and Satan works overtime to bring destruction to marriages, families, and individuals.

I also know that God weeps when we suffer.

He wept when my babysitter's husband exposed me to things no two-year-old should remember as an adult. He wept when, at age nine, my son stood over the open grave of his best friend. He wept when pre-teen and teenage kids over and over again wounded the hearts of my son and daughter.

There's so much that's out of our control. It's easy to blame God and even easier to blame other people with righteous anger in our hearts. While that anger may be justified, God has said, "'Be angry, and do not sin': do not let the sun go down on your wrath, nor give place to the devil" (Ephesians 4:26). God didn't say to never be angry. He simply said don't let your anger lead you to sin or give the enemy an opportunity to wreak further havoc.

Anger and unforgiveness are usually bedfellows. One generally accompanies the other. Forgiveness is often partnered with releasing anger . . . and anger is a powerful emotion. Releasing it or hanging on to it – they're both choices only we can make. To truly let go of the anger we feel takes forgiving the one(s) who caused it.

When we choose to let go of anger, particularly when we feel justified in it, it can sometimes only be accomplished as a determined act of self-will. When (not if) that anger rears its ugly head again and again, we get to choose again and again . . . and remind ourselves that we've let that anger go and have chosen to forgive. The more we make that conscious choice, the easier it becomes, because the enemy of our souls comes to realize that the anger stemming from whatever situation caused it no longer holds any power over us. So, he eventually stops using it as one of his weapons against us.

When our pastors' son died, it shook the very foundation of my faith in God. At first, I shoved it all down and ignored it. But eventually I had to face the anger, confusion, and betrayal I felt toward the God in whom I'd placed my faith. When I tell you it wasn't pretty, I'm downplaying it.

There was a critical moment when I was lying on my face at church, sobbing, utterly heartbroken during worship. The team was singing, "Give Us Clean Hands" by Charlie Hall. The song includes the lyrics, "Oh God of Jacob." In that moment, God spoke to my heart, "I am the God of Jacob, the God of those who wrestle with Me. Wrestle with Me and do not let Me go until I bless you."

That began a two-year journey of angrily pushing Him away and then, just as quickly, desperately pulling Him close and clinging to Him. A friend recently asked me what my first step was when I began to wrestle with God. Without hesitation I responded with, "I was a brat toward Him." I told her I railed at God and said all the things I'd never dared say to Him before . . . because I had been taught to walk in "the fear of the Lord."

I began reading books by authors like Donald Miller whose faith questions at that time so closely echoed my own inner battle. I found it gave me permission to say things to God I'd long held in. I questioned. I accused. I sulked. And, at first, I didn't really want to listen to any responses from Him.

It was in that season I learned God was big enough to handle me being irreverent, throwing accusations at Him, and asking the questions I'd always been taught you never ask God, but simply accepted as being His "will." I told God, in no uncertain terms, that I didn't want to learn anything about Him through any *man* because I was over that. He had to reveal Himself to me and personally teach me who He was and that was the only thing I would accept.

I seriously think God sat in heaven, smiled, accepted my challenge, and declared, "Game on!"

I came to know the truth of who God was during that time and I began the journey of discovering the truth of my identity in Him. That two-year process laid the foundation for what became a decade of healing that resulted in both life and faith renovation within me. It was far more than restoration. I was like a house torn down to the studs. I had good bones but, beyond that, everything had to be rebuilt. It was a time when I did nothing in church ministry. I just sat hidden in the crowd, happy to no longer be living in the fishbowl of ministerial life surrounded by countless onlookers.

Ever so slowly, new understanding dawned and my eyes were opened to revelation from Him I'd never known before. The revelation came through conversations with Him and through His Word, as well as through new friends who proved themselves trustworthy in walking with me on my journey of discovery. It was on this foundation my faith was rebuilt, as I saw God put into practice the things He promised in His Word, even through hardship. Maybe most especially during those times.

Forgiveness.

Letting go of anger.

Being real with God, knowing not only that He's big enough to handle it when we pound His chest with our fists and lash out at Him with our frustrations and disappointments, but that He loves us right where we're at and holds us close to His heart as we push and pull at Him in our struggles to understand.

These are the things that grow our faith and renovate our lives. The tearing out of things that need to go can be a painful process, but when the rebuilding is complete, what remains is far more beautiful than what had been.

Conversation Starters:

1. Ask God, "Are there any offenses I hold in my heart toward You? If so, what are they?" Then ask Him the next logical question following His answer.
2. Another good question to ask is, "Lord, who am I holding unforgiveness in my heart toward?" Then ask Him to help you forgive and release them.
3. Picture yourself holding anyone you have offense against in your outstretched hands. Give them to Jesus, pray for them, and ask Him to bless them. *"But I say to you, love your enemies, bless those who curse you; do good to those who hate you, and pray for those who spitefully use you and persecute you"* (Matthew 5:44).

CHAPTER 3

Dreaming of Greatness

The other day I was reading in Genesis and came to chapter 37, which is titled "Joseph Dreams of Greatness"[1] in my Bible. I didn't get beyond the title before a conversation began in my head.

"How many of us dream of greatness? How many of us see those dreams fulfilled?"

I didn't get any immediate answers, but the questions stuck with me for days as I continued to ponder them.

How many dreams do we have throughout our lifetimes? Some see their dreams fulfilled, but I would venture to say that, for the majority, most dreams don't come to pass. Why is that?

Sometimes, it's because our dreams change. When I was younger, I dreamed of going skydiving, but time passed without me making it happen. I got married, later started having babies, and suddenly being a mom (which had always been one of my greatest dreams) took precedence over going skydiving. I no longer wanted to take that risk. Later I became afraid of heights, so I have absolutely no future plans for skydiving! I also don't have any regrets in not fulfilling that dream.

On the other hand, I've always wanted to learn how to jump on horseback. I did it accidentally when I lived in Wyoming and the horse I was riding leapt over a ditch, but I've always wanted to jump fences and feel the strength, confidence, and courage of the horse beneath me. That's still a dream of mine, even with knees that aren't as well-suited to riding as they used to be.

Together, my husband and I have big dreams – ones that span nations, as well as dreams close to home. One of our biggest dreams is to one day own farm property with a house of our own, along with an additional structure for people who want to come and stay to get refreshed in His presence.

And . . . we'll have a big barn. Of course, we'll have chickens and an assortment of farm animals. But that barn! It will be a space for worship sessions, youth gatherings, retreats, weddings . . . maybe even a house church. I hear it being said, "Let's go to The Barn tonight!" Our property will be named "The Renovated Life" and people will come . . . so many people . . . to encounter Him and sense the immense love He has for them. I know that's a dream of His heart for us and one that will come to pass in His perfect timing.

Any of us could put our names into that Genesis 37 title: "Andrea Dreams of Greatness" or "Luke Dreams of Greatness." Luke is our oldest son and he and I are so alike in personality. He used to be a prodigal. Not only did he come home, he's now attending Bethel School of Supernatural Ministry and is growing in his faith at such an accelerated rate I can't help but be in awe of God. Neither of us is dreaming of greatness to make a name for ourselves, but we're dreaming because we both know we're called to affect change in the earth, as God works through us to establish His kingdom here. I believe God wants us to have influence because He wants us to be His voice, His hands, His feet, and He wants to give us the nations as our inheritance.

Yet sometimes, I've gotten discouraged dreaming. I've seen all that's not taken place – all that hasn't happened yet – and I've begun to wonder if it will ever happen. Then self-doubt begins to creep in, and I start to second-guess myself, telling myself that my dreams are too big, or that I'm not enough . . . and then my self-esteem tanks. I hear myself saying those dreams weren't *really* from God, they were just pipe dreams.

> Hope deferred makes the heart sick, but
> when the desire comes, it is a tree of life.
> (Proverbs 13:12)

Being "heartsick" isn't just a phrase, it's a real thing. Proverbs 13:12 is familiar to so many because it resonates so deeply with countless numbers of people. Repeated disappointment hurts the heart and batters the spirit. It can make it hard to hang on to the dreams you have and to keep dreaming.

One thing I've discovered is that, in those times of waiting for dreams to be fulfilled, God is working on me. First and foremost, He's transforming me so my heart is right when those dreams become reality. Woundedness, insecurities, needing accolades, and so much more can totally derail or even destroy us if a dream becomes reality before we're ready. God's greatest desire is for intimate relationship with us and for us to know the truth of our identity in Him. He won't sacrifice those just so we can have our dreams. He loves us too much for that.

I've also discovered that God is equipping me with the skills and capacity I'll need when my dreams become reality, so I can manage what I'll be given. As much as I've longed for years to own a farm, I haven't been ready for it and neither has Brian. It would have been a disaster in so many respects if that dream had been fulfilled before we were ready!

There's a lot we feel called to do in this world in building God's kingdom, and for some of it, it's going to take money to do it. Developing farm property, building safe houses for those who have been trafficked, and so many other things we long to do, require finances. And finances have been a huge struggle for us over the years, making that the primary source of hope being deferred in our hearts.

It's hard to share this, but when our kids were growing up, we were on food stamps and qualified for free, state health insurance for all of them, as well as free school lunches. When you're not able to meet your own family's needs, it doesn't leave a lot of margin to help meet the needs of others, plus there's a lot of shame connected with it. Still we've always been generous givers of what we have, whether we've given financially or of our time or inviting people into our home for meals or to stay with us. We believe in "Give, and it will be given to you: good measure, pressed down, shaken together, and running over . . ." (Luke 6:38). And we've experienced the generosity of God through other people countless times.

27

If you're struggling financially, here's what I would say: *Don't let what you don't have keep you from walking toward your dreams, or from starting to see them fulfilled.* Let the Lord bless the loaves and fishes you have and multiply it as you freely give. (John 6:1-14)

There's also a lot to be said about learning to be faithful with the little you have in hand *before* being trusted with more. For instance, over the years we've learned a lot about how to better host in our home and create an atmosphere that enables people to connect heart to heart with Jesus. We've learned to listen more and talk less. We've grown in intimacy with God and hear Him so much better than we used to and, because of that, we're better able to love others with His love. This has all been preparation for future dreams held within our hearts.

Because we've been willing to embrace the process of transformation in our own lives, we're far more equipped for what we know still lies ahead. Not only that, but in being faithful with the little, God knows we can be trusted with more – and so do we.

I'm sure you know the Parable of the Talents in Matthew 25:14-30. A man is heading out on a trip and leaves three of his servants in charge of different portions of his money (talents), each according to his ability. Did you catch that "each according to his ability" part? None of them were given more than they could handle. *Sometimes we want things we're not ready to handle yet and God in His goodness and love waits until we're ready.*

While the man is gone, the two servants with the most money made more money, while the servant with the least money was afraid of his master and hid the money in the ground. That seems really odd, doesn't it? The bottom line was that he was scared of the man he served (and scared of failing), so he did nothing.

How many of us are paralyzed by fear of what others will think or do if we go after our dreams? Worse yet, what if we try and fail and, in the process, disappoint God, ourselves, and those in our lives? That fear alone can keep us stuck in our tracks.

What was the man's response toward his servants? To the two who earned more he said, *"Well done, good and faithful servant! You have been faithful with a few things; I will put you in charge of many things. Come and share your master's happiness!"* (Matthew 25:21,23 NIV). The servant who did nothing with what he had, lost what he did have, and wasn't put in charge of anything.

In walking toward the fulfillment of our dreams, God gives us opportunities to be faithful with what we have, learn additional skills, and have our hearts and character transformed. God knows that, *"If you are faithful in little things, you will be faithful in large ones. But if you are dishonest in little things, you won't be honest with greater responsibilities"* (Luke 16:10 NLT).

God *wants* us to succeed, so He gives us opportunities to try and to learn. It's like a baby learning to walk. Lots and lots of steps are taken while holding a hand before that baby even attempts to take a step on her own. And, when she does, she falls any number of times before gaining solid footing, walking on her own, and eventually running. But every time she falls, a loving hand helps set her upright.

In the same way, God sets it up for us to take our first steps, initially holding His hand, then eventually taking our first steps on our own. Each time we fall, He doesn't scold us, but just sets us back on our feet to try again. *And He celebrates each step we take!*

Sometimes a child takes on an "I can do it myself" attitude and refuses that outstretched hand of help. God always gives us a choice of embracing the process or fighting against it. Oh goodness, how often I've fought the process!

Have you ever wondered why you seem to go through the same thing time after time? There can be different reasons, but one may be that God, in His lovingkindness, gives us more than one opportunity to grow. Whether it's because we've shunned the first offered chances, possibly in willfulness, or because we have further to go in our growth in conquering things that have held us back, He gives us opportunities to try again and succeed.

Maybe we still need to heal or to forgive or to let go of things we've tried to control. Maybe we need time to learn how to lean into Him more fully, growing in trusting Him to move the mountains before us, and learning how to move mountains as we speak to them with the authority He's given us in Jesus.

Out of His great love for us, He completes the work He has begun in us, and sometimes that's a process that needs to be walked out in our lives. We may need to put into practice some of the things we've been learning and growing in before moving on to the next step in our faith walk. God is so gracious in giving us more than one chance to try and succeed!

For instance, more than once we've been in the situation of needing to move to a new rental and not having the money needed for the move. At first, it was incredibly stressful to walk through it. Later, it became much easier for us when we faced it again because we knew that God had done it before, so he would do it again. We walked with faith and trust and had the grace to wait patiently for His answer to our prayers.

Rather than perceiving things as continually happening "to" you, try looking at challenges as opportunities to learn to respond instead of react, to wait patiently in trust and hope, to let go of past hurts and trauma that have become present triggers, and to surrender your attempts to control situations and, instead, turn them . . . and the dreams of your heart . . . over to the One who has a plan and a strategy far better than your own.

Sometimes we need to contend for our dreams and that can require courage. This was definitely the case for Joshua and the Israelites he was leading. In the first chapter of Joshua, we get to hear the conversation God has with Joshua, filling him in on what's going to happen as he takes Moses's place as leader of the Israelites. God tells Joshua that everywhere he puts his foot, God has given him the land and that God will be with him, never leaving or forsaking him. (Joshua 1:3, 5)

As you read on, you discover that not once, not twice, but *three times* God tells Joshua to "be strong and of good courage" (Joshua 1:6, 7, 9). They were entering the land flowing with milk and honey – the land promised to them as their inheritance and that God had already deemed as belonging to them. But they still had to rid their Promised Land of enemies. And each battle for possession of their dream required them to be strong and courageous.

God has planted dreams in your heart that He's already given you possession of. But you need to be willing to contend for them and fight the battles required to rout the enemy and inhabit your Promised Land.

What does contending look like? Often it can be positioning yourself in a place of trust and rest in the Lord as He goes before you to fill in every valley, make every mountain and hill low, straighten crooked paths, and smooth rough roads. (Luke 3:5) Sometimes it looks like taking steps of faith that look a lot like risk in the form of action, and all you can do is believe God that, as you step out, you'll walk to Him on water just as Peter did. (Matthew 14:22-33) At other times, it's simply a matter of spending time with Him because His presence is so powerful it can cause the mountains before you to melt like wax. (Psalm 97:5)

Many times, it looks like you meditating on the promises the Lord has given you, reminding Him of prophecies spoken over your life, and decreeing and declaring the truth of the Lord over your dreams. Scripture is a powerful weapon in your hand. It's sharper than any two-edged sword (Hebrews 4:12) and is called the Sword of the Spirit (Ephesians 6:17), which makes it an incredibly effective weapon in destroying the enemy. Even Jesus used the Word of God as His weapon when confronted and tempted by Satan at the end of His 40-day fast. (Matthew 4)

Contending can also take on the form of worshipping the One who has already won each of your battles and fulfilled all of your dreams, even if that fulfillment is still in the future. He's *always* worthy of praise and worship and, when we take our eyes off our circumstances and focus on Him, battles are waged and won in the heavenlies . . . and all we did was praise Him.

There's greatness within you. Keep on dreaming of and contending for it until it becomes reality!

Conversation Starters:

Before having these conversations with the Lord, listen to Rita Springer's song, "Great Defender" and position your heart to hear through worship as battles are won in the Spirit on your behalf.

1. What dreams of greatness are in your heart? Take some time to close your eyes and dream without restraint, conditions, or impossibilities, and write them down. Keep a running list and continue to add to it over time. When any of those dreams become reality, put the date next to them. Seeing those dates will grow your faith and help you stay encouraged while you wait to see other dreams come to pass.

2. Ask Holy Spirit, "Am I holding on to any disappointment in my heart that's preventing me from moving forward in faith and hope?" Write

down anything He shows you. Ask God to help you release those things and forgive anyone who may have disappointed you, including yourself.

3. Ask the Lord to show you anything you may be trying to control or are refusing His help with in fulfilling your dreams. He's inviting you to surrender to Him and accept His outstretched hand.

Endnotes:

1. Hayford, Jack, et al., editors. *Spirit Filled Life Bible: New King James Version.* Thomas Nelson Publishers, 1991.

CHAPTER 4

Recalibration - Getting in Sync with Him

God has been talking to me about His timing a lot recently and it makes Isaiah 55:8-9 roll around in my mind.

> "For My thoughts are not your thoughts, nor are your ways My ways," says the Lord. "For as the heavens are higher than the earth, so are My ways higher than your ways, and My thoughts than your thoughts."

When I've questioned God's timing on things in my life, it's often left me questioning God Himself. It's made me wonder if He *really is* good? Does He *really* love me? *Really* care about what I'm going through? If He did, then He'd certainly understand when I have time-sensitive needs and am left utterly confused and feeling abandoned when He doesn't seem to answer my prayers (read "guttural cries for help") in time.

I *know* His thoughts and ways are higher than mine and He has a perspective I don't have. But when we've faced eviction, had utilities shut off, or didn't have much food for our family that day, it's truly made me wonder, and it's caused me to not only question Him, but to lose faith in His goodness, provision, and love. Have you ever felt that way in the midst of circumstances you've faced?

Over the process of time, and especially more recently, I've come to realize more than ever that my concept of time is incredibly lacking. I know God created time and I've often heard it said that He stands outside of time. But what does that really mean?

Each of us has a certain number of days on the earth. Sometimes days that turn into weeks, then months, and even years can feel like an eternity, while other times it seems like they're over in the blink of an eye. I think it's safe to say that, for most of us, the older we get, the faster time seems to fly by, while it felt like it moved slow as molasses when we were younger.

For us, the early years with our kids seemed to go by slowly. But then, suddenly, it was as if we'd blinked and our kids were driving, then going to college or around the world on a nine-month mission trip, and now two have gotten married. I just want time to slow down, maybe even stand still for a bit. Let me catch up to all of the swift changes. Plus, there's still so much I want to do in this life and I've already passed that 50-year landmark birthday!

If we stop to think about our time here on earth as compared to spending an eternity with God, and if we factor in that time has been passing for four billion years or so, we realize our lives here are just a blip on the screen. And the times we feel are long periods of waiting aren't even a second on an eternal timeline.

It shifts perspective, doesn't it?

God sees the end from the beginning and, before we were even born, He knew us, called us by name, and had written our names in His Book of Life. As the Creator of time, He really does stand outside of it.

He separated night from day, and He causes the sun to move across the sky from east to west. He's determined the amount of sun and darkness for each day and established the seasons. He created the units of time by which we live our days in hours, minutes, and seconds. Fun fact – did you know that all clocks are calibrated to a lump of cesium atoms located in Boulder, Colorado?[1] How do the atoms know the time? Because they were created by the God who called them into being and created time itself.

I think one of the greatest examples of time not lining up with expectations was the Israelite's 40 years in the desert. It was a trip that should have taken them 11 days. Unfortunately, they made some pretty major mistakes along the way, including lack of belief in God's promises, as well as creating a golden calf to worship instead of God, and that caused their rather epic delay. (Exodus 32)

Moses was the Israelites' leader at the time, and when he was gone for 40 days, meeting with God on top of Mount Sinai, the Israelites thought he wasn't coming back. They determined that since they'd apparently been abandoned by both God and Moses, they'd take things into their own hands and come up with a solution. (I'm sure you remember how well that worked out for Abram and Sarai in Chapter 1.) Since God was seemingly MIA, the Israelites went ahead and created a god of their own to turn to, *in hopes that what they created would rescue them.*

Ouch. That hit a little too close to home. How often have I determined my own plan of rescue and created a "god" of my own to come through for me? I'm pretty self-sufficient and resourceful. I can't even count the number of times I've come up with a plan or solution, put all of my focus and energy into making it happen, believing that what I created would be THE thing that would turn things around in my circumstance . . . AND had it fall flat – lifeless and useless. Kind of like the Israelites' golden calf . . . or the idol Dagon that fell flat on its face on the ground before the ark of the Lord, head and hands broken off. (1 Samuel 5:4)

I once had a friend remind me that anything I put my focus, attention, time, and effort into more than God was an idol. She was referring to my continual focus on our family's financial survival. *How* were we going to make ends meet? *What* could I do to make that happen? *When* could I fit in additional work to bring in extra income? I would literally lie awake at night planning and scheming instead of praying, worshipping, and celebrating Jehovah Jireh, the Lord Who Provides. I wasn't seeing God move in time, at least according to my understanding of it, so I was going to be the savior we needed through the work I could produce. I.D.O.L.

It's pretty easy to judge the behavior of the Israelites, until you realize how closely it resembles your own. How many times have I ridiculed the Israelites for their "stupidity" when I've done the same thing, just in a different way? The answer to that question is "countless."

Even after their massive failure (i.e. sin), we see in Exodus 33 that God still wanted the Israelites to go forward to the land He had promised them. He wasn't going to go back on His word, but He also wasn't going to go with them. He'd send His angel with them instead. Their stubbornness and sin had created a divide between them and God. God had pursued them and shown Himself faithful, good, and powerful, but they had offended Him with their behavior and wounded His heart.

Far outside the camp, Moses set up a tent as a meeting place with God. It needed to be a good distance from where the atrocity of sin had occurred. The people watched from a distance and saw God, in the form of a pillar of cloud, meeting and talking with Moses. They knew God was still with them, but there was a separation between them and God due to the sin they had committed. So, they chose to worship Him from a distance. (Exodus 33:7-9)

How often do we allow the sins we've committed to keep us from drawing near to God? The Israelites were perfectly fine with keeping God at a distance and allowing Moses to meet with Him in their stead. They were afraid to draw near because they knew what they had done and, because of that, they missed out on the relationship they could have had with God – one that could have been deep and intimate. Instead, they let shame and fear of consequences become lines of separation.

We do the same today. We run and hide from Him, staying at a distance because we're afraid of Him and ashamed of ourselves, just like Adam and Eve were ashamed in the Garden. In the midst of our fear and shame, we forget Jesus died and rose from the grave in order that our sin would be forgiven and that the relationship God longs to have with us would be restored. We can draw near to Him . . . even when we've sinned.

Repentance and the forgiveness we receive restores us to that place of intimate relationship with Him, yet we run and hide, believing it's better to stay away, distanced from His heart.

Because of the depth of friendship Moses shared with God, he knew God's heart and was able to have the most incredible conversation with Him. It was there Moses told God that if God's presence didn't go with them – the entire nation, not just Moses – then Moses didn't want to go any further. The cry of Moses' heart was, "If Your Presence does not go with us, do not bring us up from here" (Exodus 33:15b). Ultimately, God granted Moses' request.

There's so much in this story, but let's focus on this single aspect: the idea of not taking a step forward without God going with you and waiting on His timing for taking those steps.

Exodus 40:36-37 says, "Whenever the cloud was taken up from above the tabernacle, the children of Israel would go onward in all their journeys. But if the cloud was not taken up, then they did not journey till the day that it was taken up."

There are more details on this in Numbers 9:15-23. What struck me most is found in verses 21 and 22,

> "So it was, when the cloud remained only from evening until morning: when the cloud was taken up in the morning, then they would journey; whether by day or by night, whenever the cloud was taken up, they would journey. *Whether it was two days, a month, or a year* [my emphasis] that the cloud remained above the tabernacle, the children of Israel would remain encamped and not journey; but when it was taken up, they would journey."

When I read "whether it was two days, a month, or a year," I broke down and cried at the recognition of my tendency to get outside of God's timing because I think things should be different than whatever I'm experiencing. Waiting is *so* hard, especially when it seems like forward movement toward the promises of God should be happening, which is even more true when there's an earthly time deadline involved!

If you're someone like me who tends to take charge and make things happen in life, is rather driven, and can figure out and implement solutions to challenges being faced, waiting can feel like it's going totally against the grain. There's a very real struggle within as far as knowing if what you're doing is trying to take steps forward in faith and stewarding what you have in hand, or if you're actually trying to *be* the solution and create the outcome.

Control needs to be relinquished. Trust and faith in God need to be exercised and grown. You have to be willing to let go and wait, whether it's two days, a month, a year, or longer. That can be *really* hard!

God, we don't want to move forward without You, and we want to be in Your timing!

I recently had an encounter with the Lord in which I saw a wizened clockmaker sitting at his workbench, precision instruments in hand, bent over the inner workings of a clock, making tiny adjustments.

I heard the Lord say that the clockmaker was recalibrating the cogs and gears so they would not only work better, but would also get in sync with the correct time, accurately synced to the time that is now.

We may get outside of God's timing, but He's able to get us back in sync with Him.

If we allow Him, God will recalibrate us to be in perfect sync with Him. Times and seasons change. If we're going to stay in tune with the current time, recalibration is needed because the times don't remain what they have been.

Cogs and gears are interconnected inside of a clock and the movement of one is interdependent on the movement of the ones on either side of it. Even when the first is calibrated perfectly, if the next is stuck or refuses to move forward, it prevents the first from moving and functioning as it was designed to and also keeps the ones after it from being able to move and function properly, causing each to get stuck in place, not able to discern the time.

However, if each cog allows the calibration, then they each move in sync with the others and they move as one. Then they're synced with the exact time God has set forth in the world.

We're all connected. Recalibration isn't just about you as an individual. It's also intended to be a recalibration with others around you. Our willingness to allow the Lord to fine-tune us affects the calibration of those we're connected to. Will we permit the adjustments or remain stuck, refusing to move forward and inhibiting others from getting in perfect sync with Him?

The Lord drew my attention to the fact that, in this vision, the clockmaker wasn't removing everything from the clock, taking all the pieces apart, working on each of them, then putting them back together. He wasn't making huge changes, just tiny tweaks.

When you calibrate something, it can mean "carefully assessing, setting, or adjusting" (according to Oxford Languages via Google.com). The Lord isn't asking us to make major changes. He's inviting us to assess and adjust where needed, making small changes that will result in recalibration, getting us in sync with the time that is now and with the beating of His heart.

Getting us in sync with the current season and time that we're in can sometimes mean waiting, either because we've tried to move ahead when God has stayed stationary, or because the timing for our breakthrough is a cog that's connected to someone else and God is setting things up for doors to be opened, provision to be made, and breakthrough to come.

Sometimes we experience rapid acceleration as He aligns us with our eternal timeline. That often occurs after an extended period of waiting that may have been a result of delays we caused through decisions we made, including ones in which we chose not to take action or follow His leading.

Can we trust Him enough to wait, and even have peace during the waiting, because we know the truth of His lovingkindness toward us?

Can we let go of controlling situations, circumstances, outcomes, and even people? Can we refrain from creating an idol out of our own efforts? And can we focus on the One True God who stands outside of time and sees from a far different perspective than our limited one? All because we KNOW He always and only has the best in mind for us?

Can we prepare our hearts, making them ready for the "suddenlies" of acceleration God wants to bring into our lives?

Can we embrace His process and develop a relationship with God that's marked by deeper intimacy than we've ever known as we have conversations with Him?

Can we draw a line in the sand, decree and declare, "If Your presence doesn't go with me, I'm not taking a single step forward," and then wait until His presence leads us?

Lord, recalibrate us to be in sync with You.

Conversation Starters:

1. Ask God to show you a time when you got out of sync with His timing and what He wants you to learn from that. Journal what He reveals to you.
2. What promises are you currently waiting on? Ask the Lord if there are any ways you're trying to be the solution and create the outcome.
3. In what ways does the Lord want to recalibrate you to be in sync with His timing? Ask the Lord what small tweaks He would like you to make in your life so you can be in time with the beating of His heart.

Endnotes:

1. Stromberg, Joseph. (2012, March 9). How Do Some Clocks Set Themselves? [online]. <u>Smithsonian Magazine</u>. Retrieved from https://www.smithsonianmag.com/science-nature/how-do-some-clocks-set-themselves-119830601/

CHAPTER 5

Hello, My Name is God

In the years that followed the wrestling I did with God, greater understanding began to dawn in my heart, mind, and spirit. For me, it began when I realized how much I had relied on my pastors and others in my life to spoon-feed me their interpretation of God's Word and perspective rather than searching out knowledge and understanding for myself. Once I stopped looking to them to be a type of middleman between God and me, I became far more adept at hearing God's voice, and I came to know the truth of who God is at a far truer and deeper level.

Don't get me wrong. I wasn't closed off to being in community and I still actively learned from others, allowing them to be iron sharpening iron with me. I simply shifted from being spoon-fed to foraging for my own spiritual food. In other words, I was no longer reliant on an individual or two to determine what I was learning and when I was ready to learn it. I went after getting to know God for myself and found ample food to feed my spiritual longings. It was like God was providing manna for me in the desert and having ravens feed me by the brook. (Exodus 16 and 2 Kings 17:2-7)

During this time, Brian and I became good friends with a couple, Peter and Masha, who walked with us (and still do), teaching us how easy it can be to hear from God, and how to further the conversation by asking God questions.

Putting that into practice has almost felt like a game between God and me – in the most playful sense of the word. God has led me on a path of discovery with a breadcrumb trail that's made it easier to follow after Him with each question I've asked. I've found treasures, in the form of greater revelation and understanding, all along the way, which has only made me want to continue on this "crumb-y" path.

Here's the thing. God *wants* to be known by each one of us. Love is always His highest goal (I Corinthians 13:13) and He pours that love out in relationship, which is why He went to such great lengths to restore the relationship that was lost in the Garden of Eden. God longs for us to know Him better and more fully with each passing day, and the more we get to know Him, the more we realize there's so much more we get to learn about Him.

In no way does that feel defeating and it never produces a sense of failure. It's like a couple who have been married for decades and still learn new things about one another, because they realize their spouse is ever growing, evolving, and transforming. So, who they get to know today is different than who they knew the day before. That's exciting to realize!

In similar fashion, while God is the same yesterday, today, and forever, (Hebrews 13:8) there's depth to Him we simply can't fathom in our limited time on earth. But that means that each day we can look forward to getting to know something new about Him, knowing we'll continue to learn more about Him throughout eternity. When I think about that, I feel such incredible excitement stir within me!

Have I gotten answers to every question I've asked? No. Do I understood the ways of God completely? Absolutely not. However, I can look back and see how much I've grown, both in faith in Him and in understanding of His character. I asked God to prove Himself to me and teach me about Himself and I haven't been disappointed in His abundant willingness to do both in my life.

Once I've gotten real revelation about an aspect of His character and grabbed hold of it, I've then become unshakeable in it. For instance, when I truly grasped that God is *always good* and believed it from the depths of my spirit and soul, no matter the pressure I was under at the time, I could still stand on the truth of what I knew about Him and not fall prey to blaming Him for struggles I was enduring.

That means I also realized I wasn't a victim anymore. I'd had the head knowledge that I have power and authority in Christ but, when it became truth in my spirit and soul, I was transformed by it. *I* choose how I respond in my words and in my actions in every situation and circumstance and with every person in my life. No one else makes that decision for me. That's both powerful and convicting. And while I've come a long way in responding instead of reacting, I still have plenty of buttons that get pushed. We're each a work in progress, right?

I want to speak this truth over you. "You're not a victim . . . at the hands of others or of your circumstances." I declare those words over you and, as I do, I pray you believe them, that you begin to grasp how powerful you are in Jesus, and that you gain a level of freedom that's an upgrade in the authority you walk in.

As our faith and understanding grow, He begins to unveil new depths in Him and invites us to "seek first the kingdom of God and His righteousness, and all these things shall be added to you" (Matthew 6:33). As I've sought to know Him better, He's invited me to learn more about so many things, including how to walk in the authority He's given me, my identity in Him, the Holy Spirit, the gifts of the Spirit, the prophetic, healing, angels, the Courts of Heaven, operating in the spirit realm, interpreting dreams, what it means to have dominion on the earth, and so much more.

All of this is just the tip of the proverbial iceberg! It really excites me to think of all that's awaiting me as I lean into His heart even more and continue to learn and grow in my knowledge and understanding of Him each day! What about you? What do you want to learn more about – either of Him or His kingdom?

I believe the best way to get to know God is through His love letter to us – the Bible. It may seem hard to understand sometimes but, if you're new to it, start in the Gospels: Matthew, Mark, Luke, and John. Those books will help you get to know Jesus and get to know God, in light of the New Covenant created through the redemptive work of the cross and Jesus' resurrection.

Through the Gospels, and the New Testament books that follow, we begin to discover that God is a God of love, not of

punishment as so many still believe. Jesus said He only did
what He saw His Father do (John 5:19-20) and everything
Jesus did was motivated by love. His responses to Mary
Magdalene, the Samaritan woman, Zacchaeus, the ten lepers,
the widow whose son had died, the woman with the issue
of blood, Lazarus, and so many others, reveal His love and
acceptance of *all* who came to Him.

Yes, Jesus got angry with the Pharisees and Sadducees for the
weight of the law they placed on the shoulders of others.
That's because He loved those who had been placed under
that unnecessary burden and knew it wasn't from God's heart.
The Pharisees and Sadducees were claiming to be the voice of
God to His people, but they weren't speaking His language.

Jesus also got angry with the money changers and those who
were buying and selling in the temple. They had no regard
for the fact that they were doing these acts in the house
created for worship of the One True God and Father of all
mankind, and that the ground on which they were standing
was holy. Instead, they bought and sold on that holy ground,
often cheating people out of their money in the process. In
overturning the tables of the money changers and driving
out all who bought and sold there, Jesus was defending the
heart of His Father and returning His house to the purpose
for which it was created – worship and prayer. (Matthew
21:12-13)

Any time Jesus became angry, it was because His anger was
ignited by love – for people and for God. It was very much the
same with God in the Old Testament. God longed to draw
near and be in relationship with the Israelites but, time and
again, they chose law over relationship, out of fear, and out of

an unwillingness to live their lives set apart for Him. Instead, they turned to worship idols they could see and touch, rather than placing their faith in the unseen, one, true God.

Their choices brought consequences that often resulted in judgement. If we don't read the Old Testament through God's lens of love for His people, we can see Him as being harsh and punitive in response to their repeated rejection of Him. This then sets us up to create a New Testament, post-crucifixion, and post-redemption perspective that's still utterly founded on law.

What does that look like? It looks like religion.

(I'm about to step on some toes. Sorry, not sorry.)

Recently, I was chatting with our daughter-in-law. Somehow, I had missed that before she was Catholic, she had been Baptist. My response to her in hearing that was, "No wonder you became an Atheist!" She burst out laughing and said, *"RIGHT?!"*

Let me back up a bit.

I always hoped each of our children would only choose to date (read, "court") a "nice, Christian boy or girl." That didn't happen with any of them, and they've all stayed away from the "courting" concept like it was the plague. Just to clarify – our definition of courting may not be what you've seen on television.

When we shared the courting concept with our kids, it was the idea that they would focus on growing a friendship with the person they were interested in, hanging out together around other people so they could really get to know each other better before establishing a heart and soul connection with them. Then, if they believed the person might be their future spouse, they would take the next steps forward in courtship from there.

We didn't promote having chaperones on dates, but we believe that "trying on" relationships and knowing you can easily end them can set people up for a potential pattern in the future in which a marriage could be considered "disposable" if it just didn't work out. That may sound a bit radical to you, but we never forced it on our kids. They knew our perspective and we allowed them to choose what they preferred.

When Haley came into our lives and our son Noah told me she was a professed atheist, my heart sank a bit. This was not this momma's "best" choice for her son. *However*, I heard the Lord speak to my heart, "Just love her." So, I did.

As I got to know her, I learned she had come from a Catholic background and discovered that she still carries some wounds from that time in her life. Through our conversations, I came to understand why she was an atheist. It actually made perfect sense to me.

I also knew she'd never been introduced to the Jesus I know and God's invitation to love her was His pursuit of her heart through me. What an honor to partner with Him.

That December, Noah explained the Christmas story to her and why we celebrate it, and she experienced a Christmas season with us like she'd never experienced before. Then, on

Easter, she stood next to me in church as we were singing songs all about "the blood." I realized she had no understanding of what that was all about and, seeing it through her eyes, I understood how horrific it all sounded. So, I explained each stanza as it was sung, and her understanding of the meaning of the cross and Easter grew through it.

Fast forward several months to when she was in college and she shared with me that she'd "said that prayer" she and I had talked about. She and Noah weren't actually dating at that time, but she and I had remained close, with his blessing. All I had done was walk with her in everyday life. In the process, God pursued her heart. She saw the way our family lived our lives in faith, with Jesus at the center of everything. She experienced His unconditional love and began to understand her identity in Him.

Rules, legalism, and religion had pushed her away. Love had won her heart.

We could have put our foot down and told our son he wasn't allowed to "date an atheist," but I'm so thankful we didn't! I don't even want to fathom how different life might be right now if we'd done that! It would have driven a wedge between us and our son and it would have pushed Haley away, validating her feelings about what it means to be a Christian, making her feel more condemned and rejected by those who profess to love God. They likely wouldn't be married, and I don't even want to think beyond that because I adore our second daughter!

If we're going to truly understand the heart of God toward us, we have to understand that He's a God of *love* – so much so that He sent His Son to endure a horrific death on the cross so He could take the punishment of our sins on Himself, redeem us, and restore us to right relationship with God the Father. It's all about love. It always has been.

I fully believe it's a well-thought-out assignment of the enemy that prevents us from being able to accurately discern the true heart of God toward us, leaving us in a place of shame for all the times we've sinned and missed the mark of what we believe He expects of us. We're constantly waiting for the other shoe to drop and for punishment to rain down on us as we wait in fear of the "Almighty God." That's not who God is, nor is that His response to us!

So many of us carry wounds in our hearts from parents and others who have been in places of authority in our lives, including church environments. These are those who punished us out of "love" and gave affirmation only when we measured up to their standards, demeaning us when we didn't, undergirding within us a "works mentality" for acceptance.

What's a "works mentality"? It's believing that if you do enough good or right things, then you'll earn God's acceptance, forgiveness, and redemption. But being a good person simply means you're a good person – not that you've earned God's love, mercy, and grace.

News flash: Jesus didn't agree with the Pharisees and Sadducees in His day, because they were the ones forcing the people to live according to laws God had never even set forth for them to follow. Not only that, but most were hypocrites who found ways to not follow the laws themselves, but instead justified living "righteously" in a self-serving manner, all in the name of God.

By the way, that's still often true in church circles today where there are plenty of modern-day Pharisees and Sadducees placing heavy, religious and legalistic burdens as yokes on the shoulders of their congregants and fellow believers. It's a major reason why people believe God is harsh, why they leave church, and why many see such hypocrisy in the lives of so many of today's Christians.

Too many church leaders and believers say one thing and then act another way, excusing their behavior while throwing stones at others whose sin is somehow deemed as being worse. Sin is sin and I'm pretty certain Jesus would be just as angry with today's Pharisees and Sadducees as He was back then.

If you've been someone who was metaphorically "stoned" by those who should have viewed you and your situation through the redemptive eyes of the cross and helped you find hope, I'm so very sorry. If you were "walking wounded" and were wounded even more by Christians who should have come alongside you and helped you heal . . . again, I'm so, so sorry. That's not how Jesus would have responded to you and it's not how Christians should respond either. On their behalf I ask you to please forgive us – whether "we" be pastors, leaders, or fellow believers.

Why am I so aware of this? Because I've been hurt and I've hurt others, all in the name of Jesus. Brian and I have actually gone back to many of those who were a part of ministries we led in the past and asked their forgiveness for ways we wounded them. Our hearts had been right, and we were doing what we believed we were being led by God to do. But we had no idea how wrong we were at times, how we absolutely didn't have God's heart toward people in some situations, and, in those instances, we didn't represent Him well.

Sometimes we acted like Pharisees and when we recognized that fact and realized we had hurt others in the name of "love" and "righteousness," it utterly broke our hearts. After asking God's forgiveness, we felt compelled to ask forgiveness of those we'd hurt. We needed to own our mistakes and do what we could to bring healing where we'd caused pain. That simple act helped them shift perspective, enabling them to begin to heal and to capture a more accurate picture of God's heart, love, and character.

Obeying God doesn't happen through following a set of rules and doing penance and shaming yourself when you make a mistake. Obedience is birthed out of the love you have for God and not wanting to hurt His heart or dishonor him through your words and actions. The more you fall in love with Him and allow Jesus to live in and through you, the more you naturally reflect Him, which is the image in which you were made, and you naturally begin to look less and less like the world around you.

The New Covenant set forth two commandments for us to follow. That's it. As stated by Jesus, they are:

1. "'And you shall love the Lord your God with all your heart, with all your soul, with all your mind, and with all your strength.' This is the first commandment" (Mark 12:30).

2. "And the second, like it, is this: 'You shall love your neighbor as yourself.' There is no other commandment greater than these" (Mark 12:31).

It's really *that* simple. First and foremost, love God with all that you are; secondly, love others. When you do both of those things, you align your heart with the heart of God. Notice the lack of rules and regulations to follow? Notice that both commandments are founded on love and relationship?

Did you also happen to notice that the love you pour out on others stems from how well you first love yourself? That's a topic for another day, but, for now, suffice it to say that if you're having issues in the relationships in your life, start working on that by looking at how well you love yourself (or don't).

Look around you. God is introducing Himself to you in myriad ways. Follow the trail of breadcrumbs He's leaving for you. I bet those breadcrumbs will often look a lot like little kisses from heaven – reminders of His incredible love for you and affirmations of your true identity in Him. Don't be surprised when He nudges you to take off any religious or legalistic glasses you may be wearing (we all do) and recognize the very real possibility that you just might be filtering your perceptions of yourself, the people, and the world around you through religious lenses, judging without even realizing it. If He lays it on your heart to ask forgiveness from someone, do it. You'll both be so glad you did!

As you get to know God better through His Word, worship, and spending time in His presence, you're going to more fully discover the truth of who He is. And I bet His goodness is going to surprise and delight you!

Conversation Starters:

1. As you spend time in God's presence ask Him, "What do you love about me?" (Remember that His voice will always reflect the Fruit of the Spirit. It's Him speaking when the words are filled with love.) Follow up that first question with, "Why do You love that about me?" and write it down.

2. Ask the Lord, "Are there any ways I've misperceived, misjudged, or blamed You for things that weren't your fault? If so, how?" You may see a picture in your mind or get an impression or hear Him speaking within you. Journal whatever you hear, from revelation to affirmation, because He may show you ways you've been off in your thinking, or He may tell you what an awesome job you've done in capturing His heart! Just know that if He reveals to you any ways you haven't seen Him in a true light, He's quick to forgive and He's inviting you to really get to know Him!

3. Ask Jesus, "Are there any ways I've misperceived or judged those in my life? If so, show me who they are." A good follow-up question could be to ask Him if there are any steps He wants you to take in moving forward, particularly if anyone He's shown you is still in your life.

CHAPTER 6

The Wind Blows

How do you feel when the wind blows around you? Is it refreshing? Uplifting? Bothersome? Frightening? Is it fun?

Wind can be a gentle breeze that kisses your face or a force that tears down, leaving a path of destruction in its wake. You can't tame it or determine where or how it's going to blow. It can be friend . . . or it can be foe.

After Jesus was carried up to heaven following His resurrection, His disciples stayed in Jerusalem, as He had instructed, waiting for the power from on high that He had promised. (Luke 24:45-53) That day came and, as they were together, a sound came from heaven that was like a mighty, rushing wind, and it filled the entire house where they were staying. (Acts 2:2)

No wind like this had ever blown through the earth before. It was more than the movement of air. It was living, breathing, and transformative, landing like divided tongues of fire sitting on each person present. The very person of the Holy Spirit came upon them and they began to speak in languages they never could before and didn't even understand – all because the Wind, the very breath of God, filled their lungs and burst forth in speech.

The Wind blew and none of them were ever the same after that.

I know what it's like to have the Wind blow in your life and never be the same again. Let me share a bit of my story and explain.

I was actually born Jewish, not Christian, and was named "Amtzah" in the Jewish temple after my birth. (Amtzah means "courage." I've said for years that God named me from the start what He knew I would need in my life.) My mother's side of the family was Jewish. Daddy had converted from Catholicism to Judaism when he married her. As I mentioned earlier, they were divorced by the time I was two. Daddy remarried when I was three, and my older sister and I gained three stepbrothers.

Our blended family began attending a Lutheran church when my sister got involved in their high school youth group. She and I were baptized Lutheran when I was seven years old, a fact I later found out very much angered my biological mom and one that really meant very little to me either way at the time. I had little understanding of faith, religion, or baptism because I'd been taught very little about any of it.

From then on, we attended church services regularly, sang in the Christmas cantatas as a family, and generally lived like hell the other days of the week with lives that weren't honoring Jesus. We were church attenders but had no relationship with Jesus, because no one ever told us there was more to faith than just attending church and participating in a few activities there.

I remember when I was in sixth grade and a "weird" family came over to our house to spend time with us. Why were they "weird"? They were *Jesus freaks* and we had no grid for understanding them. Our family had never encountered a family like theirs before and we never wanted to again! Yet, there was something so different about them that I've never forgotten them, even to this day.

By the time I was in middle school, we'd switched to a local Methodist church because Daddy got offended by something that happened at the Lutheran church. About the same time, Momma started listening to Moody Bible Institute Christian radio station, which the rest of us hated.

My parents became concerned about the crowd I was hanging out with in my public school. So, when my sister suggested a change in school environments, my parents thought it was a good idea, and I found myself attending a Christian school. It was there I was introduced to what it means to have a personal relationship with Jesus – a concept I'd never heard of before then, and I found myself being surrounded by "Jesus freaks." The thing is . . . they didn't seem so freakish now. They seemed loving, kind, and accepting. And I was drawn to it.

On November 6, 1981, a classmate helped me pray a prayer in which I asked Jesus into my heart. *And the Wind began to blow in my life.*

Being in a Christian school at the time made those two earliest years of growing in my faith "easy" because I was surrounded by Jesus in everything I did. All of my studies were founded on Christian principles, I had to memorize the books of the Bible, was tested on weekly scripture memorization, and even prayed before and after every volleyball game we played as a team.

I also continued to go to the Methodist church we were attending, but no one there ever talked about having a personal relationship with Jesus or about "asking Him into your heart and surrendering your life to Him." I sang in the choir, did lots of solos over the years, and attended youth group after we moved to a new town where Daddy was appointed a judge in our county.

Then I started public high school, where no one talked about their faith, or following Jesus, or living their lives for Him. I was desperate to be accepted in my new environment and Jesus faded into the background as I dated, snuck out and drank with my friends, and got involved in the theater world, performing in a variety of productions.

I didn't feel the Wind blow, or, at best, I ignored it when it tugged at my heart.

I graduated early, after my junior year, and that summer before college I found myself attending a charismatic Catholic youth group. I'd never experienced anything like it before! I went away on a youth conference weekend with them and still consider that a landmark weekend in my Christian walk. I had an experience on the bus ride home when I was praying for a girl and had no idea that what I was praying through with her was actually her going through deliverance.

The Wind rushed through that youth conference and through me. I was on fire for Jesus in a way I'd never been before, but I didn't really grasp what I had experienced, and I left a few weeks later to go to college in Wyoming, where I was on my own to figure it out and stay firm in my faith. I was now living in Mormon country and many of the Christians I encountered really did seem weird to me. So, without a church and a supportive community, my new-found freedom of being out from under Daddy's strict rules meant sneaking into bars at 17 and joining in on the party lifestyle to make friends, fit in, and have fun.

There may have been wind whipping around the mountains in which I lived, but the Wind was quiet and still in my life at the time.

By the time I was twenty, I had moved to Connecticut where I was living as a nanny. That's when I met the man who would later become my husband. It was also when I began to understand the experiences I'd had with the Wind. Brian brought me to his Spirit-filled Episcopal church (where we were married two years later) and I listened to teaching about the Holy Spirit. People were baptized in the Holy Spirit, prayed in tongues, and had gifts of the Spirit active in their lives.

I didn't fully understand what all of this was, but the Wind was blowing . . . and I was hungry to fully experience it!

It was there I learned that asking Jesus into your heart as your Savior and being filled with the Holy Spirit were two different things, and those two were also different experiences from being baptized in water. I had this insatiable desire to understand everything and it wasn't long before I prayed to receive the baptism of the Holy Spirit . . . and the Wind gently brushed my cheek with a kiss.

It wasn't what I had expected.

Throughout my life, I've struggled with perfectionism and the need to do things "right," so when I prayed to receive the baptism of the Holy Spirit and tongues didn't just flow out of me like the "rivers of living water" that had been explained to me, and instead I only got a couple of syllables as my prayer language, I questioned if it had really "worked" for me.

I still started praying in the Spirit using the two syllables I had been given to utter, hoping that, as I did that in faith and obedience, my prayer language would grow. I hid in my bedroom that I'd rented from an older couple at church and I would *whisper* those two syllables so that I wouldn't be heard, because I was embarrassed at how inept I felt like I sounded. I *wanted* this, so I was willing to not give up until it really flowed as it did for everyone else I knew. I had a strong community I could turn to for support, which helped, but the enemy still tried to discourage me and get me to quit, whispering his lies of doubt in my ear. He nearly succeeded.

But . . . the Wind continued to blow and, like a kite that struggles at first to get off the ground, I ended up soaring on the heights of the Wind and it's carried me ever since. That was just the beginning of the Wind blowing ever more increasingly in my life, bringing me to greater depths in my relationship with God – depths that before I'd been baptized in the Holy Spirit I'd never realized I could access.

Every person's experience with the Wind of the Spirit is different. Why did I share mine with you? Because the Wind, that same Wind of the Holy Spirit from centuries before that's still available to us today, was an aspect of my Christian walk I didn't know existed to me as a Christian. Maybe you didn't know that either. Maybe, like me, you've never had anyone mention it to you, or if it was talked about, it was from the perspective that it was only for the disciples and the people of their time, but not available to us today.

I also shared my story because the aspect of speaking in tongues didn't come easily to me at the start. If you've tried in the past and given up, thinking it just wasn't a gift given to you, I want to encourage you to try again and keep praying whatever syllables come out of your mouth. Use what you have and, like the Parable of the Talents, more will be given to you. (Matthew 25:14-30)

The Christian walk without the Spirit lacks a depth of intimacy with God that He longs for us to experience with Him. When you're filled with the Spirit and you pray in the heavenly language you're given, you're speaking His language. And while you don't understand it intellectually, your spirit knows (1 Corinthians 14:14) and you're connecting spirit to Spirit with the One who redeemed you and called you by name.

There will be times when you may not feel anything when you pray in the Spirit, but you're not what you feel, and what's happening in the spirit realm when you pray isn't the sum of what your emotions are telling you. Mountains move in the Spirit. Faith grows. Battles are won on your behalf. Doors are opened and others are closed as they're meant to be. Divine strategies that you need to overcome and succeed are downloaded.

Praying in tongues can enable you to hear the voice of God more clearly throughout your day as you start to recognize His voice speaking within you and begin to understand what He's saying. It also gives you access into the spirit realm, where God dwells, and as you press into His presence and lean into His heart, you'll often sense His nearness and be drawn in even deeper by His love.

If this is all new to you, I do want to clarify something that can be a little confusing. There's a difference between tongues that you pray out as your own personal prayer language – a gift to everyone baptized in the Holy Spirit – and the Gift of Tongues, which is a prophetic gift that's done in a corporate setting and is always followed by an interpretation in your known language, either by you or someone else. Both are still present and active today.

There are plenty of books written about tongues and the distinction between one's personal prayer language and the Gift of Tongues, and even more disagreements in the body of Christ related to the subject. Honestly? It's not an argument worth having. The question I would ask is what's the fruit you're experiencing when praying in tongues?

Yes, you may struggle at first in the same way I did. But if that happens, once it becomes easier, are you experiencing greater spiritual growth? Is your understanding of Him increasing? Are you developing greater intimacy in your relationship with Him? Are you sensing His leading and recognizing Him at work in your life more than you did before? When you face challenges, have you been able to walk in greater faith, trust, and authority in Christ as you pray in the Spirit and surrender it to Him? Have you been able to find a place of peace in Him in the midst of chaos you may be experiencing? Have you ever suddenly known the direction you should head in and the next steps you should take after praying in tongues? Those are God's strategies and blueprints for you that He's downloading to you in the Spirit!

Here's another way to look at the person of the Holy Spirit. He not only came into the world as Comforter, He's also the power aspect of God. (Luke 24:49; Acts 1:8) The One who moves mountains does it through the power of the Holy Spirit. Without that power at work in and through your life, you'll continue to have a mountain that obstructs your view of what's on the other side. Some mountains we're meant to climb (Exodus 19) while others are meant to be removed and cast into the sea. (Mark 11:23-24)

Wind can turn mountains into dust. That's a researchable fact. It might take a couple of thousand years, but it can happen. For God, one day and a thousand years are totally interchangeable. (2 Peter 3:8) For us, that "day" can sometimes feel like it's never-ending, but there's often more mountain-moving progress being made than we even realize. And, at some point, we look out in the same direction and that impossible-looking mountain that's been looming before us has either become totally scalable or has been entirely moved out of the way.

You want the Wind to blow and move the mountains you're facing!

In my mind, if God's got something for me, I want it. His Word says to, "Pray passionately *in the Spirit,* as you constantly intercede with every form of prayer at all times. Pray the blessings of God upon all His believers" (Ephesians 6:18 TPT, emphasis mine). That's not a request. It's a directive from God and one I want to follow.

Not only that, but the Holy Spirit is one-third of the Trinity. Why would I want to miss out on an aspect of God that's so significant? It would be like telling my husband to share two-thirds of himself with me, but keep one-third of himself tucked away, because I don't want to know or experience that aspect of him, because I'm not sure if that part of him is for me and it might even scare me a bit. When you think about it that way, it's crazy!

So, friend, *let the Wind blow in your life!*

If you've never experienced the Baptism of the Holy Spirit and spoken in tongues before, today can be your day if you'd like it to be! Your walk with the presence and power of the Holy Spirit comes after you've asked Jesus to be your Lord and Savior. If you've never done that before, it's simple!

Romans 10:9 in *The Passion Translation* says, "And what is God's 'living message'? It is the revelation of faith for salvation, which is the message that we preach. For if you publicly declare with your mouth that Jesus is Lord and believe in your heart that God raised him from the dead, you will experience salvation."

Not only that, but 2 Corinthians 5:17 (TPT) says, "Now, if anyone is enfolded into Christ, he has become an entirely new creation. All that is related to the old order has vanished. Behold, everything is fresh and new."

Take a moment and simply pray,

> Jesus, I believe that You are Lord, that You came into this world as Savior to redeem me from my sin, and through Your death and resurrection, You have restored a right relationship between God and me. Thank You for forgiving me and making me a new creation in You. My life is Yours."

Now, tell someone you've prayed that prayer and share with them your exciting news!

Are you ready for the Wind to blow in your life?

Receiving the power and infilling of the Holy Spirit is not about your efforts but *is founded in your faith of having received Him*, just like when you receive Jesus into your heart as your Lord and Savior. Luke 11:9b tells us to "ask, and it will be given to you; seek, and you will find," so all you need to do is ask.

> Jesus, You sent your Spirit to fill us with Your power, enabling us to do the works You did while on the earth and even greater, according to Your Word. Send Your Spirit to fill me now. Holy Spirit, I

ask that you come upon me and baptize me, filling me with Your power and anointing. I receive this baptism in the Spirit by faith and believe that because I've asked for it, I've received it.

Now comes the fun part! Begin speaking out whatever comes out of your mouth. Don't think about it! Remember, this doesn't have to do with your intellectual understanding and reasoning. This is *His* language you're speaking.

Here's something super important to keep in mind: the Holy Spirit doesn't move your mouth for you. You get to take a step of faith and begin to speak. The Holy Spirit meets you in that place of faith and gives you the utterance. You may experience an incredible flow of words that are unknown to you or you may utter a couple of syllables over and over like I did. Use what you've been given and use it often! The more you pray in the Spirit, the more you grow in faith and in your relationship with God, and your prayer language will flow and sometimes even change.

I'm so excited for the adventure that's ahead of you as the Wind blows in and through your life!

Conversation Starters:

1. Remember when I shared that there were times in my life when I ignored the Wind of the Spirit blowing in my life or that the Wind had seemed stilled because, at the time, I'd pulled away from my relationship with God? Ask the Lord, "Are there any ways I'm currently hindering the Wind

from blowing in my life?" Then ask Him what the next steps are that He wants you to take.

2. Sit with the Lord and close your eyes. Ask Him to give you a picture of ways He wants the Wind and power of the Holy Spirit to blow in and through your life, perhaps moving mountains in your life, your community, culturally, and in any areas of influence He's given you. Journal what He shows you and speaks to you. You might even draw it out. Look at this as part one of a continuing conversation and ask Him more about it as He leads you.

3. Spend some time praying in the Spirit. You decide for how long. Then, sit and begin writing whatever comes to mind as you remain in God's presence. If you don't know where to begin, start by asking God, "What's on Your heart today?" Then begin writing. If you get stuck again, ask another question. Don't judge what you write. Just let your pen move across the page, writing down whatever comes to mind. When you feel like you've finished, go back and read through it to see what God spoke to you. I bet you'll be surprised and delighted! This is a great way to practice hearing from God and you'll grow in it the more you do it!

CHAPTER 7

Now What?

Jesus is in your heart, fire has ignited your spirit . . . now what? Oh, my friend, the adventure has only just begun! There's so much more awaiting you!

Throughout the world today, the blind see, the lame walk, the deaf hear as countless people pray for those around them! Food multiplies in answer to faith-filled prayers, and thousands of orphans are fed through the work of organizations such as Iris Ministries in Africa. The dead are raised by people like David Hogan, Robby Dawkins, and others. Young and old alike are having visions and dreams. Seeing the angelic is a regular occurrence and operating in the Courts of Heaven is normal.

Can you feel the excitement? God is up to powerful things in the earth today. He's doing it creatively, and He's partnering with people like you and me to accomplish His plans throughout the world!

Seeing what God is doing today has made me think a lot about what happened through the lives of Bible greats like Moses, Elijah, Elisha, Peter, John, Enoch, Philip, and others.

When I do, my spirit begins to ignite within me, because I get an even greater sense of what God wants to do today, in our time, through *us*.

Take a moment to think about it. These are just a few of the things God did through these men of old . . .

- Moses parted the Red Sea.
- Elijah called fire down from heaven on the prophets of Baal.
- Joshua had time stand still.
- Elisha raised an ax head from the bottom of the Jordan River, purified poisonous soup, caused an abundance of oil to flow from a single flask, and raised a woman's son from the dead . . . just to name a few.
- Among other things, Peter walked on water and was brought out of a locked jail cell in the middle of the night by an angel!

Enoch, John, and Philip? They were *so* cool! Enoch walked faithfully with God and then "was not, for God took him" (Genesis 5:24). He was *that* close to God that God wanted Enoch to be *with* Him, so He simply took Enoch from Earth. There's *no record* of Enoch's death!

John was caught up to the third heaven and didn't know if it happened when he was in his body or out of it. All he knew was that he was in Paradise and heard inexpressible words man isn't allowed to hear. (2 Corinthians 12:2-4) That experience caused him to pen the Book of Revelation!

Philip was directed by the angel of the Lord to go speak with an Ethiopian eunuch and help him understand Isaiah's prophetic words in light of Jesus having fulfilled those words. After Philip explained the text to the eunuch, the man believed, was baptized by Philip in the Jordan River, and then Philip disappeared and found himself in another city about *34 miles away!*

It doesn't say anywhere in the Bible that those kinds of miraculous, supernatural acts were to ever stop happening. So, *we* should all be expecting to walk similarly today!

Elijah, Elisha, Peter, John, Enoch, Philip – all were normal men who were no different than you and me. They weren't "super humans," nor were they perfect. Bless Peter and his brash ways! I *so* relate to him. Despite his many failings – not the least of which was denying he knew Jesus at the time of Jesus' inquisition – he was forgiven, restored, and went on to be a cornerstone in the founding of the early church. If God could do great things in His kingdom through *Peter*, He can do them through *anyone*, including *me,* and including *you!*

That knowledge has given me a lot of hope throughout my walk with Him. No matter our failings, He can still use us and, just as He has throughout all of time, He often works through the most unlikely people. No sin is greater than another and redemption doesn't happen on a sliding scale. Sin is sin. And when you're redeemed, you've been forgiven, with your sin being remembered no more by God. (Hebrews 8:12) None of us is disqualified in a kingdom founded on love, mercy, and grace!

We *may* not be translated like Philip or cause time to stand still like Joshua, but there's no reason why it couldn't happen. God and Jesus are one and the Word says Jesus "is the same yesterday, today, and forever" (Hebrews 13:8). When Jesus lives in us, He lives through us. Each of those miraculous acts occurred in *His* power, not the power of man. So, if He's living and working through us today, why wouldn't we expect to partner with Him in the miraculous?

Some of Jesus' last words spoken on this earth were, "'Most assuredly, I say to you, he who believes in Me, the works that I do he will do also; and greater works than these he will do, because I go to My Father'" (John 14:12). What "greater works" is He going to do through *you*? I can give you a hint. He left us with specific instructions to help us get started: "Heal the sick, cleanse the lepers, raise the dead, cast out demons. Freely you have received, freely give" (Matthew 10:8).

Did you notice there are no caveats in that scripture? He didn't say, "Those I've called and anointed, heal the sick." Nor did He say, "Those who are gifted, raise the dead." Neither did He say, "Those who are trained, licensed, ordained ministers, cast out demons." He didn't even lay out a requirement for the length of time you have to have been a Christian before doing these things! *He just told us to do it!*

I know I'm stepping on toes saying this, and that I'm breaking through some mindsets founded on religion rather than relationship, but when Jesus tells us to do something, He'd like us to obey. We choose whether we're going to or not.

Unfortunately, the church is extremely divided on many theological beliefs, including those related to the supernatural and miraculous. Many denominations believe that tongues and miracles, such as healing the sick, raising the dead, and casting out demons, ended with the deaths of the Apostles, because they were the only ones directly told by Jesus to do these things.

Did Jesus ever say that only the Apostles would fulfill this mandate? Did He ever put a time limit on these miraculous acts and say it was solely for a particular time in history?

He didn't.

So, why are the majority of Christ-followers on this earth not doing what He asked us to do? I think there are several reasons . . .

- We hold fast to wrong belief systems, such as miraculous deeds ending when the Apostles left this earth.
- We believe if it's for today, it's only possible through those who have training, knowledge, great faith, or a public ministry.
- We're afraid of "failing," so we don't even try.
- We prayed for someone once and it didn't "work," so we believe we haven't been given that "gifting" or calling.
- We believe we're being arrogant if we think we can do what Jesus did.
- We have the perception that if God doesn't work in a specified manner we've predetermined (read "fits in the box we've created for Him"), then it's not by

God's hand and it must be a false spirit or prophet we were warned not to believe in. (Matthew 7:15-20; 1 John 4:1-3)

My question to you regarding that last point is, "What's the fruit you're seeing?" Do these miraculous and supernatural acts point to Jesus and give all glory to Him? Do they draw people closer to the heart of God and cause them to believe in the truth of Jesus as the Savior of the world? Does the person who is praying for the sick, raising the dead, and casting out demons profess it's solely by the power of God and not of themselves that these miracles are occurring?

Take a moment and ask yourself if you're seeing God do the miraculous through *you*. If not, do any of the reasons above resonate with feelings you've had? I know I used to hold many, if not all, of those beliefs.

When I did grab hold of the revelation and understanding that God still does miracles today, and that they're not meant to solely be done through a few of His "chosen ones," but that He wants to do them through *me*, I was gripped with fear.

You see, I don't like to fail, and I certainly don't like to look foolish in front of people. I also didn't want to be seen as one of *those* people who were weird and made claims in Jesus' name and had nothing happen when they prayed. I didn't want to scare people away from God because of my ineptitude. I didn't want to try and then be faced with the realization that I didn't have enough faith for the miraculous to happen through me because, if I did, then obviously I should see the mountain in front of me move instead of having things stay the way they were before I prayed, right?

Do you see how self-focused I was in each of those statements? I made it all about me when, in fact, *the miraculous has nothing to do with me* – outside of me being God's hands and feet for doing what *He* wants to do in people's lives.

I don't perform miracles. *God* does. Once I stopped putting the pressure on *me* and hid myself in the Miracle Worker, then I had the courage to take a risk, step out in obedience to His leading, and step into the miraculous. All He needed from me was my "yes."

Robby Dawkins often says, "How is faith spelled? R.I.S.K." Yep! When you step out in faith, you're taking a risk and you're trusting that God Himself will hold you up!

Peter walked on water because Jesus told him to come and Peter placed his trust in Jesus to make it happen. He knew there was nothing he could humanly do to enable himself to walk on water. But because he'd been with Jesus and knew Him intimately, Peter knew he could trust Jesus. He knew that as long as he kept his eyes on Jesus, he could do whatever Jesus asked of him, including walk on water. (Matthew 14: 22-33) It's no different with us!

Healing the sick, raising the dead, casting out demons – *it's not about you.* It's about Jesus and the power and authority He wielded when He defeated Satan through His death and resurrection, then turned around and empowered us with His Spirit to do even greater works than He had done while on the earth. It's *His* authority we walk in when we pray!

Before being taken up to heaven after His resurrection, Jesus spoke to His followers and said, "All authority has been given to Me in heaven and on earth. Go therefore and make disciples of all the nations, baptizing them in the name of the Father and of the Son and of the Holy Spirit, teaching them to observe all things that I have commanded you; and lo, I am with you always, even to the end of the age" (Matthew 28: 18-20).

Did you catch the last part? "I am with you always, *even to the end of the age*" (verse 20, emphasis mine). Jesus knew the disciples wouldn't still be alive on earth at the end of the age. So, He wasn't just speaking with them. He was seeing into the future and was talking directly to *us* in this statement. He's with us and He's telling us to do the same things He told His disciples to do!

So, how do we walk this out?

Just like Peter walking on water, it's as simple as taking one step, then another, keeping your eyes on Him the entire time. It's being willing to take risks, trusting that He'll do what He promised in His Word He would do. With each step you take, your faith grows. You learn not to give up and, pretty soon, you begin to see mountains move.

For me, this has been a journey founded on spending time in His presence, reading His Word, worshipping, listening to teachings, and reading amazing books on all kinds of topics including healing, the prophetic, the supernatural and miraculous, angels, the Courts of Heaven, and so much more. Then I've had to walk out my newfound understanding in real life.

The Bible says, "Faith without works is dead," (James 2:26b) so that means I need to put action to what I'm believing. I've had to take risks, step out in faith, *and actually pray for people and prophesy*, believing that God *will* show up and work and speak through me.

When I do pray for people, I always remind myself that it's not about me. I'm not causing something to happen. I lean into Jesus, remember who He is, and what His love made possible for each one of us:

> Yet He was the one who carried our sicknesses and endured the torment of our sufferings. We viewed Him as one who was being punished for something He Himself had done, as one who was struck down by God and brought low. But it was because of our rebellious deeds that He was pierced and because of our sins that He was crushed. He endured the punishment that made us completely whole, and in His wounding we found our healing. (Isaiah 53:4-5 TPT)

I know that "With men this is impossible, but with God all things are possible" (Matthew 19:26b). So, it's from that place of understanding, faith, and authority that I ask people if I can pray for them for whatever their need may be in that moment.

I might pray for healing, needed provision, or for another creative miracle, such as breakthrough in finding a new home, having a baby, or for a family's prodigal son or daughter to return home. Sometimes I find myself speaking prophetically over the person. Sometimes it's waging war for them in the midst of their battle. With each prayer, I'm believing for Him to do the miraculous, and I've seen the miraculous happen more and more as I've put action to my ever-growing faith.

Praying for someone to be healed has been my biggest step of faith and an area I'm still growing in. It used to be that when someone needed healing, I would pray a quick prayer and *hope* it worked. I didn't ask if they noticed a difference and, if it wasn't obvious they were healed, I just left it at that, told them that some healing needs to be walked out, and we went our separate ways.

Why did I do that? Because, at that time, I didn't have an accurate theology based on a true understanding of God's healing power. I had built a theology around what my experience had been. Not only that, but I didn't know there was a better way than how I was going about praying for healing for people.

I also had this idea that unless the person was jumping up and down because of having been totally healed right then and there as a result of my prayers, I had obviously failed or didn't have the "gift of healing." (Again, wrong theology.) I didn't want to face the possibility that I had failed or to have the person feel disappointed in God on account of me. (That would have been awful!) So, I tended to leave the healing prayers to those with a track record of success.

The very first time I prayed and saw someone healed from something "big" was when I was on a mission trip in the Dominican Republic. While on an outreach up in the mountains, I prayed for a little boy who was deaf in one ear. No one was more surprised than I was when his hearing was fully restored!

The crazy thing is that, even after having had that miraculous experience, it didn't cause me to turn around and pray for everyone I saw who needed healing! I continued to pray for people here and there and saw a few people get healed of minor things. But because I still believed healing to be a miracle that happens sometimes, but not all the time, I didn't pursue it in the way you would think I would have after seeing the miracle happen with that little boy.

My theology and understanding of God's plan for healing needed to be changed in order to see a change happen in me.

And just how did that happen? I dug in with God and asked Him to teach me His truths regarding healing. He led me to others I could learn from who had a far better understanding and greater faith in this area than I had and, through them, I began to discover the power and authority I walk in as His daughter. I learned that praying for healing for someone *is all about enforcing the victory of the cross in the lives of people on the earth!*

As I learned more about God's desire to heal, I also discovered that some of the beliefs I'd long held about God – such as the idea that He would "put sickness on someone" to teach them a lesson, or punish them for something, or use it to somehow draw them closer to His heart – were completely wrong.

What kind, loving, *good* Father would do that to His child? Sickness is *not* a gift or a punishment from Him! God only wants *good* things for His children! I know that may really challenge some strongly-held beliefs, but ask Jesus the truth about it and see what He says.

As my faith and understanding have continued to grow, so has my expectancy for people to be healed when I pray. I'm called to heal the sick, raise the dead, and cast out demons in Jesus' name, so I keep praying in faith. The more I walk in the authority He's given me when I pray, the more I see the miraculous take place. I've never prayed and had someone raised from the dead yet, but I know people who have, and I know it's possible. One step after another . . . and the mountain *will* move!

Have I prayed for people and not seen them get healed? Absolutely! But I'm okay with that because I know it's not about me achieving or failing. It's about me following Jesus, obeying His mandate to heal the sick, and that it's by His power, not mine, people are healed.

It's also not my responsibility to defend or protect God's reputation and character. If I pray and someone doesn't get healed, I'm not reflecting poorly on Him. I'm representing Him well by loving the other person enough to pray for them and believe with all the faith I possess that He *will* heal them!

Sometimes grabbing hold of someone else's faith and experience grows your own faith to believe for the same. One time, I was at a friend's house and mentioned that I needed to get an adjustment at a chiropractor. Her response was, "Wanna see something? Come here!"

She sat me down in a chair, knelt at my feet, checked the lengths of my leg, saw one was shorter than the other, then prayed and commanded my leg to grow out. I thought she was crazy, but then watched in utter amazement as my leg literally grew out to the length of the other! As a result of my friend's prayers, God did a divine adjustment in my body, evening my legs out in length!

The following Sunday, I shared my testimony at church. Our pastor asked if anyone there had the same issue I'd had. Three people raised their hands, so my pastor had me go pray for each of them. With each person, I literally watched and felt their shorter leg grow out to the length of the other as I was holding both legs in my hands! Grabbing hold of my friend's faith and having had the experience I did gave me the faith to believe the same could happen as a result of my own prayers!

My faith for healing and the miraculous skyrocketed after that, and my perspective shifted even more. I began to walk in greater confidence and authority as I prayed with the faith *of* Jesus, rather than just faith *in* Jesus. When you pray with the faith *of* Jesus, you see mountains move!

I've seen God do some amazing miracles in response to prayers I've prayed. It doesn't mean I'm someone "extra special" or "extra anointed." I'm just a regular person who knows God and the love He has for each of us, and I know that *nothing* is impossible with God. (Luke 1:37)

The important thing to know is . . . *there's no difference between you and me.*

What's the next step you're going to take in faith and what miracles will you then see take place? Healing is just one of the things God is doing around us each day. What else might He want to do through you? What if you began your day asking God, "How do you want me to partner with you in the miraculous today," then consciously looked for opportunities to pray for people wherever you go throughout your day? It's pretty exciting to think about, isn't it? I'd love to hear your amazing stories!

Conversation Starters:

1. What is your personal philosophy on healing and the miraculous taking place today? What do you believe about it being possible for God to do it through *you*? Ask God if there are any ways He's inviting you to change your perspective and journal what comes to mind.

2. Ask God what beliefs or fears you may have that may be obstacles to your walking a supernatural lifestyle in which you see God doing the miraculous through you on a regular basis.

3. Take a moment to dream with God. Ask Him, "What miracles do You want to do through me?" Journal whatever He speaks to you or shows you. Go back regularly and reread this entry to build your faith and celebrate what you see unfold in the days to come.

CHAPTER 8

His Perspective, Not Ours

I'm sure you're familiar with the saying, "Hindsight is 20/20." How many times have I shaken my head, thinking, "If only I could have known years ago what I know now!"

Part of me thinks I would have done things differently if I had known what would come from the decisions I made. The other part of me is so thankful for who I've become as a result of all those decisions, both good and bad, that I don't want to change a thing.

Yes, life has been really hard at times, and a good bit of that has been my own doing. But when I look through God's lens, I see redemption. I see how mourning has turned into dancing. I see accelerated growth that seemingly puts me where I should be on His divine timeline. I see "suddenlies" after decades of waiting.

With that perspective, I can have hope when I look at a mountain looming before me.

I can look at the past, remember what He's done, and know that if He did it before, He'll do it again . . . in an entirely new way.

I can have forward vision and see the future I know awaits me. I can grab on to that vision with faith-filled hands, not let go, and prophesy His promises to me.

I'll never pretend to understand why certain things happen. I can't explain away two miscarriages, after having had three perfect pregnancies, and say it's okay that it happened and that I accept it as being "God's will." I don't believe God loved my babies so much that He took them home to be with Him, or that He was saving them from deformity, disease, or disaster. I know there's an enemy who roams about the earth seeking whom he may devour (I Peter 5:8) and I believe my babies were two of his casualties.

I don't have an explanation for why God didn't protect them, but I know He wept with me, held me close in His arms, caught every tear I've shed, and let me beat against His chest in grief and anger. He spoke their names to my heart, He's given me visions of them in heaven, and I know I have the promise of eternity with them. I refuse to be weighed down by bitterness or anger and, instead, look to the future with expectation in my heart! I choose to shift my perspective and see through His eyes, rather than my own, and . . . I still believe He's our Protector!

Now that I've entered my 50's and two of our children are married, I've begun to reflect on my life. Remember I said I've realized I made some assumptions about how things would play out in our family and in our kids' lives? Those assumptions led to disappointments I didn't need to experience, and wouldn't have if I'd stopped long enough to get God's perspective.

I'm so thankful God sees the end from the beginning and nothing that happens takes Him by surprise. Just like us, our kids are writing their own stories and their faith has had to become their own. I've discovered it really is true it can be much harder for kids raised in a Christian home to remain passionate about Jesus and not go through a "falling away" period in their lives. I'd heard that from friends who had walked through it, but seeing it happen in our family shifted the beliefs I once held and opened my eyes to see things differently.

I have a salvation story I can easily recall, whereas our kids have known Jesus all their lives. They may remember asking Him into their hearts, but because it wasn't as dramatic of a "conversion story" for them, it wasn't necessarily as impactful. They've still had to go through the process of choosing to follow Jesus themselves, not just because their parents modeled it for them. As our kids have grown into adults, they've each walked their own path, and it hasn't been as neat and pretty, "all tied up with a bow," as I had pictured in my mind it would be.

Truth bomb: If I vacillated back and forth in my faith through my growing up years and as an adult, why on earth would I have thought my children would be exempt from similar struggles, especially when they saw their parents wrestle with issues that didn't seem to change despite our faith-filled declarations and stance? Why would I assume they would choose to believe in a God who seemingly didn't answer their parents' prayers . . . or their own? Why would I have thought the pull of the world would have no effect on my kids just because I've "raised them right?" I *know* how strong that pull is and how it can entice.

It's only been recently I've been able to take off my rose-colored glasses and see their faith walk for what it is – one that's no different than my own, or any other person's on earth who's been presented with the Gospel message and needs to make a personal decision whether to follow Jesus or not.

One difference that does exist between our kids' stories and my own is that their entire lives have been covered in prayer. I *know* that ". . . the prayer of a righteous person is powerful and effective" (James 5:16 NIV) and that ". . . whatever you ask for in prayer, believe that you have received it, and it will be yours" (Mark 11:24b NIV). So, I can't be shaken in my belief that the prayers prayed on their behalf have had, and will continue to have, a huge effect on their lives.

I also believe that when you "train up a child in the way he should go . . . when he is old, he will not depart from it" (Proverbs 22:6). So even if they wander, I'm convinced and have seen for myself that prodigals can return. They just roam a bit first and may come home with some scars or a limp – like Jacob . . . or maybe like their mom or dad.

Give them grace, love them well, and *remember who you know they are* – because God's shown it to you. See your children through God's eyes and be filled with hope. They can never wander where God's passionate pursuit of their hearts can't find them. As much as you love them, He loves them even more.

Love them. Continue to pray for them. Stand on every word God has spoken to your heart about them.

They will return.

Want to know how to drive them away? Be harsh, legalistic, demand they behave according to your specifications, cause them to fear your reactions and wrath, don't show mercy or offer grace, and don't listen to their hearts or be cognizant of what they're walking through. How do I know? Because I've done all of these things – all in the name of being a good Christian parent and "loving" my kids.

It's easy to forget how hard it can be to grow up and make wise decisions along the way. When we grab hold of God's perspective as we parent our kids, we begin to see how He must feel about us, even as adults. Thank goodness He's long-suffering and His heart is always focused on redemption and restoration!

God can work *all* things together for good (Romans 8:28) which means there isn't a situation or circumstance He can't redeem. Are you willing to allow God to transform the way you see your children and the choices they're making? Will you love them even if the life they're leading goes against what you believe and want for them? Can you see them through God's eyes and not try to fit them into the perfect mold you created for them?

The thing is . . . God has had a vision in mind for *each of us* from the beginning of time. We were created intentionally, with design and purpose, in order to do good works while here on earth:

> For we are His workmanship, created in
> Christ Jesus for good works, which God

> prepared beforehand that we should walk
> in them. (Ephesians 2:10)

Standing outside of time, God sees the end from the beginning and all the days in between. He knows who He's created us to become and what He's created us to accomplish, as well as the plans He has for others' lives we're to intersect with – because the life we live is about way more than just us.

When I stop to think about the countless times I've stepped away from His best plans for me, I gain so much understanding – not only for my children, but for how His heart must ache when I make decisions that draw me away from the goodness He's planned for me, or when I fight against what He's wanting to do in my life. It certainly shifts my perspective on my parenting when I think about how He's needed to parent *me*!

I look back and remember how, despite having given my heart and life to Jesus when I was 12 years old, I lost my virginity at 17 to someone I didn't even love, let alone someone who wasn't my husband. I think about how I got engaged at 19 and nearly married a man who was an abusive alcoholic. I came so close to setting myself on a path that would have forever altered my life! I remember how, at 20, I was "dirty dancing" with two guys on a podium at an under 21 club, dressed in a bra top and spandex skirt.

Then, just months later, I met my husband. And the way he saw me through the eyes of Jesus opened my eyes to be able to see how this broken, insecure girl, who'd made so many wrong choices, could *still* be deeply loved by her Heavenly Father. How I could be totally accepted for who I was in that moment in time because He still perceived me as the daughter He had created me to be and destined me to become.

If we can grab hold of the ability God has given us to see people through His eyes, we can experience a tremendous shift in the way we see the world around us, as well as our relationships. That shift includes being willing to surrender our idealized notions of what people and life "should" look like for ourselves and those we love. When we can do that, it transforms the way we respond to situations we face, particularly those involving the ones closest to our hearts.

Here's a paradigm shift to consider: What if God wants to bring revival through those who were once drug addicts or sex-trafficked or those who live "wild"? Would you believe me if I told you that's exactly what He's doing?

Never have I been so undone than when I was in the Philippines worshipping with girls who had been rescued from the sex bars in Angeles City. I was there with our daughter, Abigail, to do a two-day small business and entrepreneurial training for them, as well as attend the college graduation of several of the girls who were part of the Wipe Every Tear ministry.

Prior to starting the training, we spent time in worship. The first song played was Amanda Cook's "You Make Me Brave." Can you imagine standing in a room filled with over 70 women and girls, all rescued out of the sex trade, who were singing to the One who made them brave enough to leave that life behind, in order to create an entirely new legacy for themselves and their family line? They bravely chose to take a chance and trust these people who were offering them a home, a college education, food, medical care, and an allowance to help them care for their needs and that of their families. They were brave enough to believe it wasn't too good to be true, and they were brave enough to surrender their lives to the One who truly was their Savior in every way.

I couldn't squeak a single word of worship out of my mouth. I could only weep in adoration of the One who could love like that. I already knew these girls are the ones who will lead their nation in business, politics, education – every facet of society – and they will be the ones God will use to transform their nation and bring revival to their land. I was there to help equip them to do what they've been created and called to do. But in that moment, I was undone at the beauty of their worship and the purity of their hearts. I suddenly understood that this abandonment to Him would be the catalyst for massive transformation in their nation, because of the sheer power that came from their worship before His throne.

I gained a perspective I'd never had before, and I've never been the same. This experience is part of the reason why I can see "the wild ones" of our society leading us in revival, and why prophetic words about the "wild ones," such as those shared by modern-day prophet Nate Johnston, resonate so deeply with me.

This is God's perspective:

> But God chose those whom the world considers foolish to shame those who think they are wise, and God chose the puny and powerless to shame the high and mighty. (I Corinthians 1:27 TPT)

It's often said that God's kingdom is an upside-down kingdom. He does things backwards from the ways we would expect. Would you have thought that someone who had once been prostituted could lead revival and worship more deeply than you've ever experienced yourself? It's a major paradigm shift, isn't it?

What if we were to approach situations in our lives in the same manner, allowing God to turn things upside down? Can we trust that, as backwards as things seem, He's bringing good out of what's happening, He's working things out for our good, and His timing is perfect, even when it seemingly doesn't fall within the parameters of the circumstance? Can we worship with abandon even when it seems like everything is crumbling around us? Can we wait on Him long enough so we're able to respond in situations, rather than react? Can we believe that, "... *Eye has not seen, nor ear heard, nor have entered into the heart of man the things which God has prepared for those who love Him?" (I Corinthians 2:9)*.

I don't know how many times I've shaken my head when reading, "A man's heart plans his way, but the Lord directs his steps" (Proverbs 16:9). In case I haven't already made this clear to you, I'm a planner, as in I plan every, single, minute detail, especially when it comes to schedules, trips, business . . . and even fun. Yes, I can be flexible and go with the flow. But in the words of the inimitable John "Hannibal" Smith of the A-Team, "I love it when a plan comes together."

Let the *Lord* establish my steps? Did I mention that I'm *really good* at planning? I can see a million steps ahead and I'm adept at identifying potential pitfalls and coming up with solutions to avert any possible problem. I can get pretty much anything done and if I can't do it myself, I'll find someone else who has the skills, ability, or resources. No worries, God! *I've* got this!

Are you laughing yet? Or are you cringing because it hits a little too close to home?

Could God's plan *really* be better than my own? I've often seriously doubted that. Can you guess what that doubting usually resulted in? Delays. I know many of the delays I've experienced in my life have been a direct result of my unwillingness to let go of my plans and allow God to direct my steps.

Sometimes we're stubborn. We want things to be the way we've envisioned them, and we're unwilling to let that vision go. I've been in that place and it hasn't worked out well for me. How about you?

Are you holding on to things the Lord is inviting you to let go of? What makes you hold on to those things so tightly? I know for me it's been an issue of being afraid to relinquish control. What might happen if I "let go and let God?" That's scary!

In those moments, I've had to ask myself if the real issue is that I'm struggling with trusting God. Questions like, "What if I let go and nothing happens?" and "What if God doesn't come through for me?" roll through my mind, as I continue to hang on, usually with a vise-like grip, because I'm certain what I can accomplish in my own strength will work out better than relying on God's omnipotence.

When I'm finally able to quiet my spirit and soul and think clearly, I ask myself if what I'm feeling while I'm holding on is producing peace and joy. Because if I'm experiencing something less than that, I know it's a pretty good indication that my trying to control things isn't working out, and it's far less than the best Jesus has planned for me. All I need to do is let Him direct my steps.

How do I do that? I ask Him, "Lord, what steps do you want me to take?" Then I write down the first things I hear, ask Him the next question I may have, and do what He's shown me to do. It may be a conversation with Him that happens over a couple of days, but rather than getting all ramped up over needing to hear an answer right that second, I press into His admonition to,

> Be anxious for nothing, but in everything by prayer and supplication, with thanksgiving, let your requests be made known to God; and the peace of God, which surpasses all understanding, will guard your hearts and minds through Christ Jesus. (Philippians 4:6-7)

I choose surrender. I choose to allow Him to shift my perspective. And I choose peace. I let that peace protect my heart that's filled with emotion. And I let that peace quiet my racing mind.

Then I take it a step further. I make a conscious choice to think only on those things that are true, noble, just, pure, lovely, and of good report — that's what I meditate on (Philippians 4:8) and my perspective shifts from my life being my own to being His. Not only does my perspective shift, but my faith grows and I find myself trusting Him more and more.

There's so much peace and joy found in a shift in perspective! Are you willing to choose His perspective over your own?

Conversation Starters:

1. What have you seen God do in the midst of challenging circumstances in your life in the past? Journal about it, then ask Him what He would like to do in the midst of the circumstances you're facing in your life today.

2. Ask God, "What vision have you had in mind for me from the beginning of time and what have you always had planned for me to do while on earth?" Write down what He shows you.

3. Are there any ways in which you need a shift in perspective regarding God working through the "wild ones" on the earth today or through others who are in your life? Ask Him to show you any judgement in your heart. Let Him put His finger on any wrong beliefs you may have and ask Him to forgive you for seeing others as less than how He sees them. Are there any steps He wants you to take, such as asking forgiveness from someone you know or writing a note or a text of encouragement to someone you may have previously judged? Act on those nudges today.

CHAPTER 9

Count the Cost

Having faith to move mountains doesn't just happen. It's cultivated and nurtured as you invest time and effort into growing your faith. More often than not, you may feel like you've "failed" as the mountains you face continue to stand rather than become leveled before you. But the times you see those mountains actually move? It drives you to pursue growing your faith even more, knowing you *will* see more and more miraculous things happen as you continue to partner your faith with His power and authority!

Let's take some time to chat about two of the biggest challenges we can face in becoming mountain movers – managing disappointment and being willing to lay down wrong beliefs. Both can be painful.

Ask yourself . . . What do you do when things happen that you don't understand, and all you can do is wonder about the goodness of God and His seeming absence and/or silence? Do you just walk away and stop believing in Him altogether? I've known a lot of people who have chosen to do exactly that, and I almost walked away myself.

Maybe instead of walking away from God altogether, you decide to hold a grudge against Him and keep Him at a distance. I've definitely done that more times than I can count! What about you? Have you done that, too?

Or . . . do you believe God's angry with you, so you stay away in fear? There have been so many times in my life when I've hidden from Him, even knowing there's no place I can go where His love won't find me. (Psalm 139; Jeremiah 23:24)

I hate to say it, but there are no easy solutions. There are no formulas for handling disappointments or for dealing with wrong beliefs, and there's certainly no cookie cutter approach for facing those two obstacles. You're going to have your own road to travel, just as I have, as has everyone else I've known. Remember when I talked about wrestling with God? That's when I nearly walked away from Him. I couldn't reconcile placing my faith in a God I felt I couldn't trust. *But* . . . I couldn't NOT believe in Him either. So, I wrestled with Him . . . and I'm so thankful I didn't let Him go!

When faced with disappointment, disillusionment, and pain, you're going to need to wrestle with Him, too – there's no way around it. Whether you're trying to make sense of a situation or are questioning what you've always believed, you're going to be faced with having questions you need God to answer. What will you do when those answers don't come or they're not the answers you expected them to be? If you're going to continue to grow in your faith and be a mountain mover, you'll have to find a way to be alright with *not* having all the answers, and still be able to trust that He *is* good, despite what you're walking through.

It's so important to continue to be in His Word and spend time in His presence in worship and prayer *before* you find yourself having to face the unexplainable. Then when things don't make sense, you can still stand on truths that are steeped deeply in your spirit and soul, even when the circumstances in front of you speak loudly to the contrary or your questions seem to fall on deaf ears.

Let's be real. There will also be times when you find you simply can't continue to stand on your own and you want to give up in the shadow of the mountain. Friend, we *all* get weary in battle. It's so important to have people around you who can hold you up in the midst of the battle you're facing. That's exactly what Aaron and Hur did for Moses when they held up his arms so he could keep his staff raised, enabling the Israelites to miraculously prevail against the enemy they were facing. (Exodus 17:8-13)

We need to know who our enemy is. The idea that "your adversary the devil walks about like a roaring lion, seeking whom he may devour" (I Peter 5:8) is absolutely true. Satan is our enemy, not God. Depending on the translation you read, the first part of that verse tells us to be sober-minded, alert, vigilant, and watch – because the enemy is looking for an opportunity to strike. When he does, we need to be ready with hearts, minds, and spirits steeped deeply in God's truths, prepared to defeat Satan and silence his lies and accusations. The enemy will try to create doubt about the truth of God's character, cause offense and anger in our hearts toward God, or make us question God's very existence and power, among other things. God's Word is "living and powerful, and sharper than any two-edged sword" (Hebrews 4:12). It's one of the most powerful weapons you have in your arsenal, so you want to be ready and able to wield it effectively against the enemy!

What will your response be when you're angry with God? Because it *will* happen. Think about this – how do you normally handle being angry with someone? That's a pretty good indication of how you'll handle being angry with God. Will you blame Him? Will you storm away in offense and unforgiveness and declare that you're done with your relationship with Him? Do you know His heart and His character well enough to know, even when He seems absent or uncaring, that's not the truth?

The truth is that He's right there beside you, and the situation you're facing didn't take Him by surprise. He has a plan. Can you be alright if it's not a plan of escape, but a plan *through* the situation? One that will see you either moving that mountain or climbing it to get to the other side?

Fair warning . . . . Things may be about to get a bit more uncomfortable during this part of our conversation. Hang in there with me. I promise it will be worth it! Let's take a look at our other biggest obstacle to becoming a mountain mover as we chat about some wrong beliefs you may hold dear.

But before we do, let me first ask you this. How do you respond to someone if they're helping open your eyes to new ways of thinking that are opposite of what you believe? Do you argue? Do you get defensive? Do you become angry? I'm a judge's daughter. I *know* how to defend *my* position. How about you? Let's both commit to be open, okay?

For instance, maybe you've held the belief that when bad things happen to someone, it's because of sin in their life or because they're being disobedient and God's punishing them. What if that's wrong thinking? Unfortunately, Christians are famously known for "shooting" their walking wounded. We see people dealing with challenging circumstances and heartache and, rather than getting in the pit with them and helping them find a way out, we often gossip, judge, and turn away – exactly when they need us the most. Even if what's happening in someone's life is a result of poor choices, we can still be compassionate and walk with them on their redemptive path to wholeness.

Maybe you believe *you're* always the cause of the challenges you're facing. It's important for us to own our mistakes, but the cross means nothing if we can't be forgiven *and* forgive ourselves. I used to struggle tremendously when facing sin in my life or mistakes I'd made. It always seemed so much easier to accept God's forgiveness than it was to forgive myself. In my mind, God's forgiveness was somehow a given, while I needed to sufficiently beat myself up and punish myself before I could move on, despite the fact that Jesus already took plenty of punishment on my behalf. I had to ask myself, if God had forgiven me, which I knew He had, then who was I to *not* forgive myself? I then had to convince myself to move on *as one who is forgiven* and not as one who's waiting for the other shoe to drop in response to my failures.

If we've spent time in environments that are legalistic and have religion rather than relationship as their foundation, being presented with ideology or theology that *isn't* rooted in the legal aspects of God's Word can be particularly hard to accept, because it can seem so foreign to our way of thinking.

Just a reminder – the work of the cross redeemed us and set us free from the law, establishing a new covenant of grace. Unfortunately, many Christians throughout the ages, as well as today, still live by law, rather than grace. As a result, religion (and all of its rules) has taken precedence over redemption. While I could point fingers at particular denominations, I won't do that because, for a time, Brian and I walked with a very legalistic mindset, and we were members of a *non-*denominational church!

As I mentioned earlier, Brian and I have both gone back to so many people to ask their forgiveness, because we had inadvertently wounded them with our legalistic ideals. We placed unnecessary burdens on their shoulders as we spoke into their lives via the ministry positions we held and the mentoring we did. We set "biblical" standards for youth and adults that looked more like the mindset of the Pharisees than the heart of Jesus. We had the best intentions but had accepted wrong teaching that we allowed to shape our beliefs. Unfortunately, that resulted in us hurting people in His name. Our hearts were right, but our understanding wasn't. We had to own that and seek forgiveness, for their sakes as well as our own.

God's Word says Satan disguises himself as an angel of light. (2 Corinthians 11:14) If he's going to deceive us and draw us away from the heart of God, including through anger and offense or wrong teaching, he's going to do it in a way that's easy to fall for and not an obvious lie. He pulls us *just* far enough away from the truth to get us off track, but does it without us realizing it, because it's so close to being true.

One of the ways this often happens is by well-meaning people taking a scripture out of context and building a theology around it. Not that I'm going to address it in this book, but the oppression of women is an easy example of this happening within the church. (Kris Vallotton has written a fantastic book titled *Fashioned to Reign,* shedding the light of scriptural truth on the subject. I highly recommend it.) The truth is the role of women in the kingdom was never delegated to solely women's, children's, and worship ministries, while keeping women out of the pulpit and governmental roles within the church. Just a reminder – God's Word says that a woman will be the one who will crush the head of Satan. (Genesis 3:15) Satan knows that, so why wouldn't he do everything in his power to silence the voices of women and prevent us from fulfilling our callings in Christ?

Are you cheering in agreement with what you just read? Or is something inside of you rising up in opposition? Would you be willing to keep an open mind and learn more? Sometimes we fight against new ideas rather than seeing them as His invitation to explore and discover. Personally, I'm someone who likes to be right, so I've had plenty of arguments simply in defense of being right. In the process, I closed myself off from expanding or shifting my understanding.

Allow me to illustrate my point. One summer, years ago, our daughter went away to dance camp. Unfortunately, the camp was scheduled during the same week we'd planned to go to Florida on vacation. Abigail went to dance camp. I was faced with a week of being the only female in a house with four males. I've never been more ready for a vacation to end! The boys argued continuously, simply because they could, and sheepishly admitted to that fact when I accused them of arguing for sport. When we all got home, I told my daughter she could never leave me alone like that again!

Sometimes we treat defending our firmly held beliefs in the same way. We argue because we can, and because we want to win. I'm an incredibly competitive person. I've had to learn that conversations in which I'm being presented with an opinion that's different from my own are an opportunity to gain understanding, even if it's simply listening to hear how a person thinks or feels about a subject. It's important for us to listen to understand, and then ask God questions to discover *His* truth in the matter.

It's also important to accept that not every point has to be argued.

Being open to new beliefs can certainly stretch us and bring us out of our comfort zone. We can remain, feet firmly planted in our perceptions, or we can take steps outside of the boxes we've created. We get to choose.

Sometimes we build theologies to explain away our disappointment when we don't see healing take place, or to help us deal with and explain disappointment when prayers aren't answered or a child dies. For instance, many believe that when healing doesn't happen, it's our cross to bear and our suffering for Christ. Then they build a theology around a belief that isn't true to the nature and character of a good, loving Father and a Savior by whose stripes we *are* healed.

Sometimes things are used by the enemy to simply bring division. A hot topic (besides politics) I've seen recently circulating is whether Christians should participate in yoga or not, even when it's "Holy Yoga," because of its roots in

Hinduism. I have friends who passionately express their opinions on both sides of the argument. It's not an argument I engage in. I'm honestly not sure how I feel about it, but what I do know is there are lots of exercise options out there that I love, so I focus on those. *Sometimes, you just need to know when to walk away.* Is your belief something the Lord wants you to explore with Him further? Or is it a distraction from the conversation He actually wants to have with you? Let me share an example.

In the past I've been very cautious about exploring certain things in the supernatural realm because I didn't want to get "off" from the truths spoken in God's Word. I know the devil comes as an angel of light and I didn't want to risk being deceived. Fear prevented me from having certain conversations with others and kept me from engaging more fully with the kingdom of God on earth and the supernatural realm.

For instance, I used to think that people who believed in angels and their presence in our lives were taking their focus off God and, because of that, they were walking in error. Then in the last couple of years, I read a few books written by trusted, well-respected individuals who taught about angels' roles in our lives. That caused me to delve into the subject in God's Word to explore for myself what *He* says about angels. Equipped with greater understanding, I discovered what I'd been missing all the years prior – angels were all around me and they were constantly working on my behalf at the command of God and His Word!

I've now seen angels when I looked up into the sky, angels in my bedroom as I worshipped God, and have had angels open our front door and come into the house when a friend was praying for our family. I've seen angels during our church service and I'm pretty certain that twice I accurately recognized that the person I was speaking to was an angel.

There was one time in particular when I knew angels had powerfully worked on behalf of our family. Our youngest son, Nehemiah, had a seizure at school and stopped breathing. The nurse was about to give him rescue breaths when he began to breathe again on his own. After I had gotten the call letting me know what had happened and that he was headed to the hospital, I cried out to God as I ran out to the car. "What happened?! I don't understand! I covered him in prayer and commissioned angels to be around him, protecting him according to Your Word. *Where were they? Why wasn't he protected?*" As I later sat beside his bed in the emergency room, watching him breathe while he slept, I heard God whisper to my heart, "They *were* there. That's why he's still here." All I could do was sob in gratitude.

While this could all get twisted by the enemy and be used to pull us off track and into angel worship, our totally discounting it, out of fear that it's not biblical or not something that happens in today's world, causes us to miss out on the powerful ministry God has designed for angels to have in our lives.

Growing in my understanding and in my faith didn't just happen. It's taken work – not works. In other words, I haven't been trying to earn anything in the eyes of God. I've been putting in the efforts of a dedicated student, learning all that I can about the One who moves mountains. I read – a lot, both His Word and books authored by amazing men and women in the kingdom. I pray and, being completely transparent, could spend more time doing that. I love realizing there's an area I can press into more with Him because I recognize that it's an invitation straight from the heart of God!

I worship – and not just at church. There's nothing that brings me into God's presence more quickly than amazing worship music. There's beauty in the hymns of old, but God is still speaking, and what's being birthed in worship today is incredible! Maybe that's an area for you to be stretched out of your comfort zone. Play a modern worship song and read the lyrics. Let the music and words bring you before His throne. In that place of being in His presence, ask Him what's on His heart and what He'd like to share with you today and then journal about it. I have no idea how many journals I've filled with our conversations, my prayers, and my wrestlings with Him!

I also listen to a lot of online messages and podcasts, and not just ones that make me feel good. I like to listen to people who will challenge me and be a catalyst for continued growth, even if they're putting their finger on things in my life that need to change, including wrong beliefs. These are also the people I follow on social media and read their blogs. I want to listen to people who will ignite for me a further conversation with God and cause me to explore a topic more deeply because I want to find out for myself what *God* is speaking on the subject. I also love when I hear someone put into words the things that were formulating in my heart, but I hadn't yet fully understood. It gives me a sense of confirmation that I was on the right track and it fleshes out the things that were more ambiguous in my understanding. It's one of the ways that God leaves that breadcrumb trail I mentioned.

Admittedly, all of this takes time and effort and intentional decision-making. You might be wondering how on earth you could fit more into your already busy life. How do I do it? I fit much of it in as I'm doing other things, such as listening to a message while I clean the house, wash the dishes, or fold the laundry. We each choose how we're going to spend our time and where we're going to place our affections. There's a price to pay to become a mountain mover. It might be getting up a little earlier or choosing to turn off the latest streaming hit to spend time with Him. There have been seasons when I've chosen to keep the television off entirely and that's usually followed a season when I had been binge-watching with the best of them and I sensed God wooing my wayward heart back to Him.

Maybe it's saying no to things that are negatively affecting your spirit. Let me ask you a question I've asked myself that's helped me recognize areas where I've needed to make some changes. Is what you're listening to, watching, and who you're spending your time with drawing you closer to God or distracting you from Him and His calling on your life? At different times in my life I've found that I needed to let go of certain friendships or make changes in my music or viewing options. My spirit is really sensitive, and I've realized I need to be aware of what I'm exposing it to each day. Like a plant, is my spirit being given lots of "Son" and watered with His Word and nourished with His presence? Or is it kept in a dark place where it can't thrive?

Becoming a mountain mover is a process founded on growing our faith, and it includes learning how to manage our disappointments, as well as being willing to let go of wrong beliefs we may have held dear for as long as we can remember. That includes being willing to listen to the ideas of others and allowing them to challenge your beliefs, so you can then determine with Jesus whether your point of view is going to change or not.

It's also setting the time aside to become a scholar and a lover of His soul, as you dedicate time to learning and being transformed in His presence. You were made in God's image. As you spend time with Him, much like Michelangelo and the stone he sculpted, God will draw out the beauty hidden within your stony exterior as He chisels away all that isn't part of your true design. That isn't always an easy or pain-free process. But if diamonds are created through pressure, what an amazing treasure is being created in us by His hand! What comes forth is *beautiful* and *powerful!*

There's a cost to becoming a mountain mover – don't ever think there isn't. But it's absolutely worth it! Are you willing?

Conversation Starters:

1. Get quiet in God's presence. Ask the Holy Spirit to reveal to you any wrong theologies or beliefs you may have that He would like you to explore more, particularly any centered around a scripture verse or a disappointment or loss you've experienced. Write down what He shows you.
2. In your time with Jesus, ask Him if there are any areas of faith you've hesitated pursuing or discounted entirely. If He reveals something to you, ask Him what the next steps are that He's inviting you to take.

3. What's your time with Jesus like? Ask Him how He would like to spend time with you. Is it in His Word? Worship? Prayer? Being still and quiet in His presence? However He's inviting you to be with Him, journal what He shows you. Then make a plan for how you're going to spend more of that time with Him and follow through with it.

Check out the Resource Page at the end of the book for suggestions of authors, speakers, worship music, and more!

CHAPTER 10

The One Who Moves Mountains

Are you a mountain or a beach person? I love the beach. But hands down, whenever I'm given the option, I'm absolutely going to choose mountains, every single time! We're close enough to the mountains where we live that I can see them in the distance. And when we go, even just for the day, as soon as we start heading north, you can watch my entire body relax. A transformation takes place within me as peace and joy wash over my soul.

When I see mountains, they make me happy. I don't look at them as being formidable or overwhelming. I see them as my "happy place." So, when there's a mountain before me, it doesn't make me feel afraid. It makes me feel at home.

That being said, there's a stark contrast between the beauty of my beloved Blue Ridge Mountains and the jagged, imposing peaks of a mountain range like the Dolomites. I find peace and joy in one, while the other makes my jaw drop open at its sheer ruggedness and dramatic peaks. Peaks that look utterly impossible to scale. It's daunting to my soul.

In the same way, there are mountains we face in life that feel easier to have faith for them to be removed, while there are others that appear terrifying and utterly intimidating. In God's eyes, a mountain is a mountain and He's created them all.

> For assuredly, I say to you, whoever says to this mountain, 'Be removed and be cast into the sea,' and does not doubt in his heart, but believes that those things he says will be done, he will have whatever he says. Therefore I say to you, whatever things you ask when you pray, believe that you receive them, and you will have them. (Mark 11:23-24)

When He told us to speak to the mountain and tell it to be removed and cast into the sea, He wasn't categorizing the mountains and sorting them into ones that could be moved versus ones that would just have to stay put. Putting a spin on a Dr. Seuss classic line, a mountain's a mountain, no matter how tall!

We've faced more mountains than I can count as a couple and as a family, and some have been pretty terrifying – from near death to not knowing what we were going to feed our family that day. Some mountains we've scaled, some we've moved, some we're still facing and speaking to in faith.

What is faith anyway? Among other things, Oxford Languages via Google defines it as "having complete trust or confidence in something or someone." Faith being interchangeable with trust was a revelation to me when I began reading *The*

Complete Jewish Translation of the Bible. I saw how verses that were so familiar to me in other translations had the word "faith" replaced with "trust." It was an "aha" moment, while also being one that made me wonder why I'd never thought of faith in that light before.

To have faith in God means you have to trust Him. When you've had trust broken or abused in your life, particularly by authority figures such as your dad or spiritual leaders, it can cause tremendous hurt, disillusionment, anger, and bitterness, and it breeds a natural tendency toward distrust and questioning of motives. Those kinds of experiences, particularly if they included physical, sexual, emotional, or mental abuse, absolutely color your perception of God and your ability to trust Him and put your faith in an unseen Being. How can you believe He is good and loving if He "allowed" that to happen? I get you.

Not everything rests on the shoulders of dads but, by nature, they're the ones who are most reflective of a father relationship with God. Very few people don't have to walk through healing from "daddy wounds," whether those wounds happened intentionally or inadvertently. "Good" or "bad," our dads are imperfect and have wounds of their own that affect how they parent.

All of us are human and we all make mistakes. Sometimes, it's the words we speak that become arrows to our kids' spirits and souls. Other times, situations occur that are out of our control and cause us to miss an event that was really important to our son or daughter. It's in that moment of absence that spirits of rejection and abandonment sink their claws into our kids' minds and emotions, writing a false narrative in their memories. Others experience far worse by hands that should be loving, but aren't.

I shared a bit about my dad already. He parented with extremely high standards, with very little tolerance for mistakes or underachievement. Punishment was hefty and wielded often and, if merited, the belt was used. That being said, I knew beyond a shadow of a doubt I was very much loved. My fondest memories include watching old movies together with my head resting on his belly, which I called "my pillow." He sang "Summertime" to me at night before bed after we'd had Oreos and milk together. He also taught me the value of traditions and keepsakes. Because of those deeply steeped values, I'm known as "the keeper of the family treasures." I learned to cook by Daddy's side and, as hard as it was to be his namesake, I was still proud to be a "Dunn."

Not long after I was baptized in the Holy Spirit, God began to deal with daddy wounds in my heart that I didn't even realize I possessed. I cried from the depths of my spirit and soul throughout that process. But I really believe God addressed that issue with me first because, for me to go where He wanted to take me in the realm of faith, I needed to be able to trust Him. I couldn't do that when my interactions with Him were colored by my relationship with my earthly dad. I had been relating to God the Father with a belief that if I was good enough, measured up, and performed well as a Christian, then I was accepted. If I sinned in some way, I expected God's punishment. And I believed that if "bad things" were happening in my life, it was punishment from God. (Remember our conversation about having firmly rooted, wrong beliefs? I had plenty!)

I also thought surrendering my life to God meant that He controlled it and that I had little to no say in my life as a result. What a lie of the enemy! How do I know it was a lie? Abraham was known as a "friend of God." He enjoyed such intimacy of friendship with God that God chose to fill Abraham in on His plans for Sodom. And Abraham had such influence with God that he was able to change God's mind. The Creator of the Universe adjusted His plan at the word of a man. (Genesis 18:16-33) Moses had the same kind of influence with God, changing God's mind when He planned on destroying the entire Israelite nation following their apostasy of worshipping the golden calf. (Exodus 32)

I needed to be able to approach my Heavenly Father, trusting I would always be accepted and wanted by Him. I needed to know that His love for me had nothing to do with what I could do for Him or how closely I followed His laws. God had to replace the lies I was believing with revelation of the truth of who He is, along with the truth of my identity as His daughter, before I could walk with the kind of faith and trust that can move mountains.

This was part of the continuing renovation process God was doing within me. What had been built on top of my foundation of understanding needed to be removed. Notice I didn't say "ripped out" or "torn down." God is far gentler than that when healing our spirits and souls. What followed were years of a renovation process that drew out of me God's original design.

God identified perceptions I held of Him that weren't true to His character, and He revealed deep-seated fears I had of abandonment and rejection. He taught me the difference between religion and relationship and what it means in Ephesians when it says, "For by grace you have been saved through faith, and that not of yourselves; *it is* the gift of God, not of works, lest anyone should boast" (Ephesians 2:8-9). I learned there was nothing I could do to earn His love and forgiveness and that He had seen me as being "good enough" to love and redeem from the beginning of time.

I think the biggest revelation for me has been *really* believing God is a *good* Father who delights in loving His children and showering us with that love in countless ways. His response to me when I mess up isn't punishment. It's, "Daughter, I love you. Let me pick you up, help get you back on your feet, and help you clean up that mess you made." He lets me do my cleanup work, but He's right beside me, giving me direction and encouraging me throughout the process. That's a Father I can trust and put my faith in!

I also began to realize just how much *He* believes in *me*. Me! What a revelation to grasp that the God of the Universe believes in me and He *trusts* me, which means *He* has *faith* in *me*! He's trusted me to walk beside my husband and be the helpmeet Brian needed. He's trusted me to parent our children, reflect His heart to them, teach them about Him, and equip and prepare them for their calling and destiny. He's trusted me to grow a business that's literally changed countless people's lives – in health and finances, as well as empowering women in leadership and entrepreneurial roles. These are things that will have an impact on generations to come. He's trusted me to create a legacy in His name! He's also trusted me with His heart and sharing it with others. He's trusted me to follow His leading, even when it hasn't made sense to me, and my obedience has brought blessing into my life and into the lives of others.

I trust Him and He trusts me. That trust has grown out of developing and nurturing an intimate friendship with Him. How have I developed intimacy with God? It's happened in the same way I've developed deep, intimate friendships with those nearest to my heart.

I spend time with the person. We talk and listen to one another. As we have deeper and deeper conversations, we get to know what and how we each think, how we feel about all kinds of topics, and what we're passionate about. We begin to deeply care about what makes one another's hearts beat, and our relationship grows as we get to know one another better.

As that intimacy develops, so does the trust and faith we have in one another. This is crucial if mountains are going to be moved!

Let's look at Mark 11:23-24 again and dissect it a bit:

> For assuredly, I say to you, whoever says to this mountain, 'Be removed and be cast into the sea,' and does not doubt in his heart, but believes that those things he says will be done, he will have whatever he says. Therefore I say to you, whatever things you ask when you pray, believe that you receive them, and you will have them.

Who is speaking in this verse? Well, if you back up to verse 22, you'll read, "So Jesus answered and said to them, 'Have faith in God.'" That means Jesus is the one speaking in verses 23-24, and He told us the first step before speaking to any mountain is to have faith in God. Remember, faith and trust are interchangeable words, so in placing your faith in Him, you're trusting Him as far as what comes next.

The "whoever" in verse 23 is literally referring to anyone — you, me, a child, an older person, female, male. "Whoever" is the person who speaks to the mountain and tells it to be removed and thrown into the sea.

The one speaking to the mountain isn't Jesus and it isn't God. My friend, you and I and each one of us on the earth are the ones who are to speak to the mountain and tell it to move!

The One Who Moves Mountains is YOU!

Stop waiting on God to move mountains you've been called to move yourself! YOU say to the mountain, "Move!"

Let me step back off my soapbox for a moment and let's continue to look at these same verses, but in *The Passion Translation*. There are some important things to note in this verse that this translation brings out so beautifully.

> Listen to the truth I speak to you: If someone says to this mountain with great faith and having no doubt, 'Mountain, be lifted up and thrown into the midst of the sea,' and believes that what he says will happen, it will be done. This is the

> reason I urge you to boldly believe for
> whatever you ask for in prayer—believe
> that you have received it and it will be
> yours. (Mark 11:23-24 TPT)

I think it's safe to say we can't just blithely speak to a mountain and expect a change to take place. Moving mountains takes great faith and an absence of doubt. It takes believing that what you just said *will* happen – it *will* be done. It's so important for us to boldly believe that what we've asked for in prayer is ours, even before we actually see the answer!

Faith to move mountains isn't something we drum up. It begins with knowing beyond a shadow of doubt who you are and who He is within you, which is knowledge born out of the intimate relationship you share. You trust He is who He says He is, that He will keep His Word, and that He will respond to what you have said because what you are speaking is totally in line with His heart.

How do you know that it's in line with His heart? By knowing His Word, which reveals His heart to us. His Word comes alive in us as we meditate on it, focusing on what He's said, repeating it over and over, allowing it to become woven into our very being so that His Word becomes familiar truth within us. Speaking the Word of God to mountains carries the weight of all of heaven with it!

When we pray and tell mountains to move, we're doing it from a position of dominion, as we enforce authority that's been ours since the Garden of Eden when God told man to have dominion over the earth. (Genesis 1:26-27) When we speak like that, we're remembering who we are in Christ and the power and authority we walk in because He is within us and we are daughters and sons of God.

The very same authority Jesus had on earth is the same authority He gave us in order that we could continue to enforce the victory of the cross in every mountain of society. What do I mean by that? Johnny Enlow, Lance Wallnau, and Bill Johnson have each written books about the Seven Mountains of Societal Influence in the earth today. (See Resources) They explain that we've been given dominion over each of the Seven Mountains: Religion, Family, Education, Government, Media, Arts & Entertainment, and Business. You and I have voices of influence in these areas of our society and we've been called to bring God's kingdom into them as we speak to and enforce kingdom realities within each mountain of society.

We are today's reformers!

You don't like what's happening in the mountain of government? What are you doing about it? We've all been called to pray for those in authority over us. (I Timothy 2:1-4) Are you praying for your political leaders, whether you voted for them or not? Are you propagating division and hatred or are you grabbing hold of the heart of God, engaging Him in conversation, asking Him what steps He wants you to take in moving that mountain and affecting change, then going out and boldly doing it? Could He be calling you to a more hands-on role, either in supporting those in office, lobbying, or perhaps even running for office yourself?

Are you angry about all of the fake news being propagated in the media? Have you started a blog and are you posting well-researched articles filled with truth? Are you trying to publish them through mainstream media outlets? Do you have a YouTube channel and followers who are listening to the truths you're sharing through a podcast?

Are you just complaining or are you stepping into roles of influence and bringing reformation to the mountains God has called you to have dominion in? Or have you abdicated your role to someone else who *will* step in who doesn't have the heart of God?

No matter the mountain(s) you're called to, you'll affect far greater change through wielding *love* as a weapon than you will by posting inflammatory remarks on social media or getting into arguments at church or your workplace. *Love is far more powerful and effective!*

> Yet even in the midst of all these things, we triumph over them all, for God has made us to be more than conquerors, and **his demonstrated love is our glorious victory over everything!** . . . **I'm convinced that his love will triumph over death, life's troubles, fallen angels, or dark rulers in the heavens.** There is nothing in our present or future circumstances that can weaken his love. (Romans 8:37-38 TPT, emphasis mine)

When you make the choice to love, it opens the hearts of those receiving it. As a result, those same people will then be far more open to what you have to say as you step into your place of influence in the mountains of society, and they'll be far more responsive to change as you begin to enforce kingdom principles. Not only that, but leading with love helps the people you're influencing discover the truth of who God is and their identity in Him. As those truths unfold in their lives and are accepted, you're empowering them through love to become ones who move mountains and bring reformation to the earth. Hell can't stand against that!

We have all been empowered to move mountains. Some are personal mountains we face, but it doesn't end there. We're called to move mountains throughout the world in every realm of society. It's a part of those good works He called us to from the beginning of time. (Ephesians 2:10)

It's important to remember that victories are often won bit by bit, and faith for small victories, once won, grows into faith for moving mountains. Smaller victories might look like praying for someone and seeing them healed of a minor illness or injury. It might be speaking to a financial need and receiving unexpected provision for it. It could be releasing peace in your home prior to a family gathering and it being the best time everyone has had together in a very long time.

Speaking to larger mountains might look more like praying for a friend to be healed from cancer or for your husband to be healed from Type 1 Diabetes. It might be seeing years of financial debt wiped out or your child set free from drug addiction. It might be believing God to enable you to purchase a farm property where people can encounter the presence of God. These are mountains we've been speaking to in our own lives and we're seeing them begin to move!

Did you catch that I said we're seeing mountains *begin* to move? We have a saying at our church, "Family celebrates progress!" For us, that looks like celebrating the fact that God made provision for us last spring to move into a great rental home with a two-year lease. That home has a farm property behind it that's also an Airbnb. Every day when we hear the donkeys bray, the goats bleat, and the rooster crow, it's a tangible reminder to us of what we know is a part of our calling, and it reminds us to prophesy God's promises over our future. It might "just" be a farm behind us, but it's constantly affirming the vision in our hearts and giving us hope for what lies ahead, even if it seems impossible right now.

Each time we've spoken to a mountain and seen it removed, it's created a stronger and stronger foundation in our faith. So, when we've been faced with mountains that were far more intimidating, we've been able to stand on the previous mountain-moving victories and believe that He'll do it again at the sound of our command. That's not arrogance. That's knowing beyond a shadow of a doubt who we are in Him and that we walk in His power and authority, ruling, reigning, and taking dominion over the things of the earth, walking out what we've been created to do. We're still a work in progress, but we'll all be growing and learning for the rest of our time here on earth.

Here's the thing. God doesn't give us more than we're able to handle. Put another way, "God is faithful; he will not let you be tempted beyond what you can bear" (1 Corinthians 10:13 NIV). He wants to be certain we can steward the blessings He pours out in a measure that is manageable for us in that season. That means, for example, that even if we have a massive calling to influence the mountain of business, we'll begin to rule and reign in that mountain by first having influence as an employee or as a small business owner. We've all seen people whose lives are suddenly changed in huge ways they weren't prepared for, such as lottery winners or the winners of reality shows, and their lives are destroyed by it in the end. That's not what our loving Father wants for His children

God wants us to be equipped and prepared, able to take dominion and thrive in our calling, not become a casualty. So, He'll wait for us to be ready before giving us greater influence.

> "For I know the plans I have for you," declares the LORD, "plans to prosper you and not to harm you, plans to give you hope and a future." (Jeremiah 29:11 NIV)

There have also been times when we've had a huge mountain looming over us and we knew we didn't have the faith to move the mountain. Instead, it felt like we were being crushed under the weight of it and we couldn't see our way out from under it. When faced with circumstances like that, we've learned to invite those we trust to join with us in praying boldly, knowing the power of agreement in prayer and its ability to move mountains:

> "Again I say to you that if two of you agree on earth concerning anything that they ask, it will be done for them by My Father in heaven. For where two or three

are gathered together in My name, I am there in the midst of them." (Matthew 18:19-20)

There are times when you need prayer backup. That's not a sign of failure or weakness. You can get weary moving that mountain bit by bit. When you have someone come alongside of you, it refuels your spirit and gives you a power boost to chuck that mountain into the sea!

Sometimes it's easier to pray boldly for someone else than it is for yourself, especially when you have a similar need. When you see your friend gain victory, it builds your faith for moving your own mountains. Move mountains together and don't let go of God's promises for one another!

My mountain-moving friend, it's time for you to be a doer of the word. (James 1:22) This book is a blueprint for you to engage God in conversation, wrestle with Him, dream, make some tweaks here and there, have the Wind of the Spirit blow as you walk a supernatural life, see things the way God does, and be the one who brings God's kingdom to earth, enforcing the victory of the cross in every realm of society.

As you do that, you walk in Jesus' power and authority. You boldly speak to mountains before you. You believe you have what you've asked for and . . . those mountains move!

You're a reformer. It's time to change the landscape of the world around you!

Go move those mountains!

Conversation Starters:

1. Take some time and ask Jesus, "Are there any wounds in my heart preventing me from fully trusting You?" Let Him take you back in time, through your growing-up years. Journal what He shows you and let His love flow into any of those hurting places. Say what you need to say to Him, ask Him the questions you've needed to ask, and listen for His responses. Remember, His words will always be kind and loving.

2. Ask the Lord, "What mountains do You want me to speak to in my life and what, if anything, has kept me from speaking to those mountains before now?" If He shows you something that has prevented you previously, ask Him what to do about it.

3. What are you passionate about in life? What makes you angry, sad, or excited? Ask the Lord what societal mountain(s) He may have called you to influence that are related to those passions in your heart. Journal what He shows you and ask Him what the next steps are that He wants you to take.

RESOURCES

This is a *partial* list of people, books, music, and ministries that have helped me grow in my walk with God. There are so many amazing people running hard after Him, there's no way I can list them all! Many have written multiple books and have numerous messages available on YouTube and on their church or ministry websites. Check them out and keep growing!

PEOPLE:

Bill Johnson (He's been a huge influence for me!)
Kris Vallotton (Prophetic)
Robby Dawkins (Healing and Leading Others to Christ)
Todd White (Healing and Leading Others to Christ)
Dan Moehler (My husband's favorite for healing, intimacy
     with God, and valuing people)
Heidi Baker and Iris Ministries (Healing and the Miraculous)
Blake Healy (Angels)
Joshua Mills (Angels)
Lana Vawser (Prophetic)
Shawn Bolz (Prophetic)
Nate & Christy Johnston (Prophetic)
Johnny Enlow (Prophetic)
Jeff Jansen (Prophetic and the Supernatural)
Randy Clark (Healing)
Danny Silk (Parenting and Relationships)

Andrea L. Johanson

Jeremiah Johnson (Prophetic and Revival)
Todd and Rachel Weatherly (Prophetic, Books and Scrolls,
    Timelines)
Daryl and Belinda Crawford-Marshall (Prophetic)
Adam Thompson (Dream Interpretation)
Robert Henderson (Courts of Heaven)
Lou Engle (Revival)
Daniel Duvall (Deliverance, Spiritual Warfare)
Peter and Masha Oswalt (Prophetic and Healing, Pastors of
    ARISE:Life Church)

MINISTRIES:

Bethel Church, Redding, CA
ARISE:Life Church, Acworth, GA
Iris Ministries, Mozambique, Africa
Wipe Every Tear, Philippines
Field of Dreams Church, Adelaide, Australia
Global Fire Ministries, Murfreesboro, TN
Bride Ministries International, https://bridemovement.com/

BOOKS:

Anything written by Bill Johnson and/or Kris Vallotton
*Translating God: Hearing God's Voice for Yourself and The
    World Around You*, Shawn Bolz (He has several great
    books.)
Do What Jesus Did / Do Greater Things / Identity Thief, All by
    Robby Dawkins
*The Divinity Code to Understanding Your Dreams and Visions
    / God's Prophetic Symbolism in Everyday Life*, both by
    Adam Thompson
Robert Henderson's Books About the Courts of Heaven

Andrea L. Johanson

Jeremiah Johnson (Prophetic and Revival)
Todd and Rachel Weatherly (Prophetic, Books and Scrolls, Timelines)
Daryl and Belinda Crawford-Marshall (Prophetic)
Adam Thompson (Dream Interpretation)
Robert Henderson (Courts of Heaven)
Lou Engle (Revival)
Daniel Duvall (Deliverance, Spiritual Warfare)
Peter and Masha Oswalt (Prophetic and Healing, Pastors of ARISE:Life Church)

MINISTRIES:

Bethel Church, Redding, CA
ARISE:Life Church, Acworth, GA
Iris Ministries, Mozambique, Africa
Wipe Every Tear, Philippines
Field of Dreams Church, Adelaide, Australia
Global Fire Ministries, Murfreesboro, TN
Bride Ministries International, https://bridemovement.com/

BOOKS:

Anything written by Bill Johnson and/or Kris Vallotton
Translating God: Hearing God's Voice for Yourself and The World Around You, Shawn Bolz (He has several great books.)
Do What Jesus Did / Do Greater Things / Identity Thief, All by Robby Dawkins
The Divinity Code to Understanding Your Dreams and Visions / God's Prophetic Symbolism in Everyday Life, both by Adam Thompson
Robert Henderson's Books About the Courts of Heaven

130

The Seven Mountain Prophecy: Unveiling the Coming Elijah Revolution, Johnny Enlow

Declarations: Unlocking Your Future, Steve Backlund

Grace Over Grind: How Grace Will Take Your Business Where Grinding Can't, Shae Bynes

The Veil: An Invitation to the Unseen Realm / Profound Good: See God Through the Lens of His Love, Both by Blake Healy

Seeing Angels: How to Recognize and Interact with Your Heavenly Messengers, Joshua Mills

The Seer, James Goll

Invading Babylon: The 7 Mountain Mandate, Lance Wallnau and Bill Johnson

MUSIC: *(Worship is such a key component of growth in intimacy with God and building your faith!)*

Bethel Music (there are a number of artists, including Brian and Jenn Johnson)

Jesus Culture (there are a number of artists, including Bryan and Katie Torwalt)

Elevation Worship

Upper Room Worship

Johnathan David & Melissa Helzer

Kari Jobe

Steffany Gretzinger

Amanda Cook

Cory Asbury

Chris McClarney

Jeremy Riddle

Misty Edwards

Rick Pino

Iron Bell

Rita Springer

A SIMPLE WAY TO
PRAY FOR HEALING

When I'm praying for healing for someone, I've learned to first ask the person I'm praying for to tell me how painful it is on a scale of 1-10 so we have a starting point from which to gauge improvement. I didn't use to do that, but I've learned the importance of it for their sake and for my own. Let me explain why.

When I ask them to identify where their pain level is on that scale, we can both identify progress in healing and can celebrate and press in for more if need be. After we've identified the level the person is at, I then pray a simple prayer for healing. It's not long or shouted and I don't use fancy words. I pray the same way I talk. I declare the truths found in His Word and I pray in the name of Jesus, giving Him all the glory. It might sound something like this:

> *Father God, I thank you for Kate. I thank You that You are a loving Father who cares for His children and You are the God who heals. Right now, I release the healing power of Jesus to Kate's shoulder and declare that by the stripes of Jesus, Kate's shoulder is healed. We thank You, Jesus, for healing Kate now and we give You all the glory. In Jesus' name, amen.*

Then I ask the person to check how they're feeling and see if they notice a difference. I ask them to number it on that same 1-10 scale and tell me where they are on that scale now. Sometimes they can't put it on a scale, as is the case with things such as cancer or something else internal or intermittent, but if they can check it out and rate it, they will. Sometimes when they can't rate it, they'll still be able to identify that they felt heat or tingling or another sensation in the area needing healing and they know that it's God's healing power at work in their body.

Sometimes the issue gets worse before it gets better or the number on the scale doesn't change at all, but because I've come to know that it's always God's desire to heal, I've learned to not let it phase me in the least when I don't immediately see the results I'm believing God for in that moment.

Unless the person tells me that the pain is totally gone and they can tell that they're fully healed, with their permission, I pray again and press in for complete healing. *If Jesus prayed more than once for someone to be healed (Mark 8: 22-26), then I figure I get several opportunities!*

As long as the person lets me keep praying, I'll pray several times if need be as I continue speaking to that mountain and telling it to move. Stay aware of the leading of the Holy Spirit and sensitive to the comfort level of the person you're praying for. You'll know when you've prayed as many times as you should.

Scan this QR Code to watch a fantastic, seven-minute video by WP Films titled, "How to Pray for Healing – Heidi Baker & More" (Published August 1, 2011). It's a segment from the *Viewpoints DVD* in the *Furious Love Event Collection.*

ABOUT THE AUTHOR

Andrea's dedication to equipping others to become Mountain Movers was born out of her own faith journey. Like many, her path has been marred by abuse, tragedy, personal struggles, and includes a long stint in ministry at a toxic church. She chose to wrestle with God over all the things she couldn't reconcile in her faith and, in the process, uncovered truths about God's character and her identity in Him. From that place of understanding, her faith has grown exponentially, empowering her to become a Mountain Mover and teach others to do the same.

Andrea has a way of being open and vulnerable as she honestly shares her stories and what she's learned, which enables her to connect with readers and others she meets. She's also an educator with a passion for teaching all ages, inside or outside a classroom environment, making it second-nature for her to allow personal experiences to become life lessons. Writing, teaching, and speaking are some of the ways she's fulfilling her destiny and calling to help establish God's kingdom on the earth, and she loves doing it armed with God's great love.

As an entrepreneur, Andrea has been passionate about empowering women to succeed in business and has even had the privilege of providing business and entrepreneurial skill training to women who have been rescued out of the sex trade in the Philippines. With a business of her own in the health and wellness field, her mission remains "to love others *well* and empower them to do the same." You can learn more about what she does at www.therenovatedlife.net.

More than anything else she does in her life, Andrea loves being a wife, mom of four, and mother-in-law, as well as a fur baby momma. While Andrea currently lives outside of Atlanta, Georgia, with her husband and youngest son, her dreams are filled with a farm property where people can come encounter the presence of God. In the meantime, she and her husband, Brian, lead weekend retreats, creating a space for people to come and meet with the Lover of their Souls. Reach out if you'd like more information on upcoming events.